A PENGUIN SPECIAL

s191

CONGO DISASTER

COLIN LEGUM

Congo Disaster

COLIN LEGUM

GLOUCESTER, MASS.

PETER SMITH

1972

CONTENTS

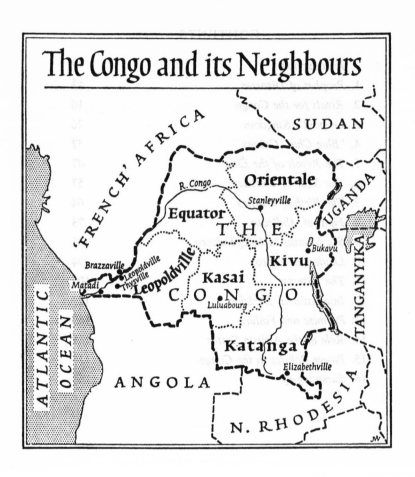

The Congo and its Neighbours

deposed Prime Minister Lumumba under house arrest, with most of his supporters in prison, and faced with an uneasy struggle for power going on within the Army.

INTRODUCTION

I STARTED this book in the late summer of 1960 to provide a background to the Congo crisis. But events have outstripped me. Already since completing the bulk of the book at the end of September the balance of forces within the Congo, Africa, and the United Nations has changed substantially. We are now faced with a new situation. While these changes do not invalidate my analysis of earlier developments, there is clearly a need to bring the last few chapters up to date. For technical reasons this must be done in the Introduction. What follows is in a sense a Stop Press, and should perhaps be read at the end of the book rather than at the beginning.

RIVALS FOR POWER

The sudden collapse of the Belgians' authoritarian power produced a vacuum which has alternately sucked and expelled various internal and external forces. In the first phase (July to September) the central power was tenuously held by a coalition between the unitarian forces of Patrice Lumumba and the federalist forces of Joseph Kasavubu, while the regional power of Katanga – the economic heart of the Congo – was held by Moïse Tshombe and the Belgians. Soviet intervention on the side of the Lumumbaists hastened the inevitable split in the coalition; this precipitated the expulsion of the Russians, and brought the first phase to an end with the vacuum still unfilled.

The second phase (last week of September to middle of November) saw a stalemate between the political contenders which opened the way for Col. Mobutu, Chief of the Congo National Army (formerly the Force Publique), to suspend parliament until the end of the year, and to rule through a '*collège d'universitaires*', later renamed the Council of Commissioners-General. Col. Mobutu acted at first as an agent of Kasavubu, but soon renounced him and at once followed Lumumba's example in alternately declaring war on, and cooperating with, the UN in the Congo. Gradually Mobutu won the support of the Belgians and of the Western Powers. This second phase ended with the deposed Prime Minister Lumumba under house arrest, with most of his supporters under UN protection, and with an uneasy struggle for power going on within the Army.

Col. Mobutu and his Commissioners-General do not figure in my assessment of leaders up to the end of September. Mobutu has been described as the 'Hamlet of the Congo'. He is intelligent and sophisticated, but constantly torn by personal conflicts. He was never a soldier, having been a clerk in the Paymaster's Section of the Force Publique. He is sensitive to criticism, and sees the UN as the paternalist successor to the Belgians. He is nevertheless willing to work with the Belgians – but strictly on his own terms. He has appointed perhaps a dozen Belgian officers and technicians as his advisors. So far, he has not succeeded in getting undivided control over the Army, nor has he yet managed to turn it into a reliable and disciplined force.

The President of his Commissioners-General is Justin Bomboka, who was Foreign Minister in Lumumba's Government (see Chapter 10). His two chief deputies are Albert Ndele, who has had post-graduate training in Public Administration, and who was Chef de Cabinet to Lumumba's Minister of Finance; and Kandolo, who was Lumumba's own Chef de Cabinet.

The third phase opened at the end of November, with President Kasavubu taking the initiative for the federalists, with the help of the Western Powers and of a substantial group of the Afro-Asian bloc. His ascendancy was marked by his right to be seated in the UN General Assembly. Relations with Col. Mobutu and the Commissioners-General again became friendly. Together they opened the offensive against the Lumumbaists by forcibly ejecting Ghana's Chargé d'Affaires, Mr Nathaniel Welbeck, in an action that led to armed conflict between the Congo National Army and the UN Forces, and by expelling other unfriendly diplomats. Encouraged by these new developments the Belgians began rapidly to return to the Congo.

The two camps – the unitarians and the federalists – are facing each other suspiciously in the next round of the struggle for power. There are two possible outcomes of this third phase: reconciliation on the basis of a federal constitution, or the introduction of the cold war through the invocation by both camps of the aid of their external allies.

THE ROLE OF THE BELGIANS

I have written sharply about the role of the Belgians in the Congo. This is not for lack of sympathy or understanding. There are Belgians who have written much more harshly than I have about their own Government's failures and about the grasping nature of Belgian financial interests which, even now, continue to behave as if their patron saint were King Leopold II.

Belgian liberals, especially at the University of Louvanium in the Congo, believe that unless Belgium agrees to work within the framework of the United Nations last July's disaster might recur with even more appalling consequences. For even though Tshombe, Kasavubu, and Col. Mobutu may be willing to work with, and to use, the Belgians, they will never again be willing to be controlled or unduly influenced by them. Unless the Belgians are capable of learning this lesson from their recent bitter experiences, they could still end up as did the Dutch in Indonesia – expropriated and unwanted. No real friend of Belgium will encourage her to continue in the policies defended by the present Government.

THE ROLE OF THE WEST

Alas for my faith in the Western leaders' genuine understanding of their best interests in Africa. While they protest their belief in Africa's development as a genuinely non-committed continent, their behaviour in the Congo is inconsistent with this aim. When, at the end of September, I was writing the chapter 'Power Politics in the Congo', I could say: 'There is no other recent example when the West played so passive a role in international affairs as it did in the Congo.'

This has since changed. The Americans now openly side with the Kasavubu camp. It may be that the federalists are right about the best kind of constitution for the Congo (personally I believe they are), but this is no justification for actively taking sides in the Congo's internal politics. Western partisanship can only weaken Kasavubu's position in the present struggle; the danger of this attitude is that it will push the Lumumbaists into the anti-Western camp and divide the West from important countries in

Africa and Asia. This is not likely to help Kasavubu, the
Congolese, or the West.

The switch in Western policy came in October, when it was
thought that Col. Mobutu and his Commissioners-General might
be able to underpin Kasavubu, and thus provide a stable alternative to Lumumba who, it was felt, could not be relied upon to
follow democratic paths either at home or abroad. Although the
Western view of Lumumba is strongly supported by many
African and Asian States, this does not make the error of intervention any less dangerous.

THE ROLE OF THE AFRICAN STATES

The balance within the group of African independent states
changed entirely as a result of the admission of Nigeria and the
French Community states to the UN in October. Until then the
so-called 'militant' African states (Ghana, Guinea, and the UAR)
held the initiative. They could count on the general support of the
'moderates' like Liberia, Ethiopia, and the Sudan; only Tunisia
was refusing to toe the 'party line' over the Congo. But the
doubling of the African membership of the UN gave the 'moderates' a commanding position; for the first time the Accra-
Conakry-Cairo axis was no longer able to exercise an undisputed
initiative. These divisions were projected into the Congo, with the
'militants' still determinedly supporting both Lumumba as Prime
Minister and Kasavubu as President; while the 'moderates' upheld Kasavubu's authority alone.

The original nucleus of the African Group (minus Tunisia)
never recognized the legality of Col. Mobutu's administration of
Commissioners-General, not even after Kasavubu had confirmed
them in office. Their Ambassadors, therefore, continued to treat
with Lumumba. They went further, considering it their duty to
give him active support while he was under house arrest. The
point at which diplomacy ends and politics begins is hard to
define. However, so long as Col. Mobutu and President Kasavubu
were too weak to exercise any effective initiative, this game could
be played merrily. It ended with the tragic showdown of force
that compelled Ghana's representative to leave the country. Thus
the divisions within the Congo have caused the explosion of the

'tensions' among the independent African States to which I refer briefly in Chapter 14. The consequences of this schism in the continental politics of Pan-Africanism remain to be seen. This part of the story is still only at its beginning.

THE ROLE OF THE UNITED NATIONS

The situation in the Congo has often been described in the past six months as chaotic or even anarchic. This is a loose and misleading description. There are some areas where lawlessness abounds, but these are the exceptions. What is remarkable about the Congo – not only about the towns, but even about the remote rural areas – is the extent to which comparatively normal life is still possible. Telephones work; cables are despatched; luxury hotels are still luxurious; the grass is still cut in the avenues of Leopoldville; trains and river boats run; internal air services operate; the ports still work. After an alarming decline, exports are beginning to show a healthy rise; the large foreign-owned plantations have hardly been affected; and most factories still work.

Of course conditions are not normal – security is constantly threatened, arbitrary arrests take place, and, worst of all, the courts no longer function. But abnormality is not necessarily synonymous with either chaos or anarchy. Apart from southern Kasai and northern Katanga, the situation has not declined into the conditions one has known in recent years in Kenya, the southern Sudan, Ashanti, the Cameroons, or Cyprus.

It is necessary to get this position into focus to appreciate the importance of the role played by the UN organization in the Congo. If there is neither chaos nor anarchy today, it is solely due to the UN operations. If the Belgians are now able to return in large numbers it is because of the security provided by the UN forces. If the Congo has, so far, avoided being swept into the arena of an armed conflict between rival foreign Powers it is owing to the UN presence. These successes overshadow all its weaknesses and failures.

In my last chapter I have described what I consider to be the mistakes made by the UN. I am not sure that any of these mistakes could have been avoided at the time. Nevertheless, they must be examined if one is to consider the basis of future UN policy in the Congo, and if similar interventions by the UN in other parts of the world are to benefit from the experience gained in the Congo.

Since I wrote the last chapter of this book, Mr Hammarskjöld has himself voiced two of the criticisms which I make. In a letter he addressed to Mr Tshombe on 8 October, he listed three factors that endanger the future of the Congo – the confused and disquieting situation which still prevails at Leopoldville; the continued presence of a considerable number of Belgian nationals; and the unresolved constitutional conflict, threatening the unity of the Congo 'which is symbolized by the name Katanga'.

'Among these factors,' he wrote, 'I regard the last two as of crucial importance, even from the standpoint of the first: that is to say, if we could fully circumscribe the Belgian factor and eliminate it, and if we could lay the groundwork for a reconciliation between Katanga and the rest of the Territory of the Republic of the Congo, the situation at Leopoldville might very well be rectified. The way towards a pacification of the country would thus be opened.'

Recognition of these two dangers leaves only one of my major criticisms unanswered: the failure to take timely action to disarm the Force Publique. In the changed circumstances this has become much harder, perhaps even impossible, unless the Army itself splits – in which case to disarm it would become imperative. But from my discussions with leading members of the UN in the Congo it is clear that they now fully realize how differently things might have worked out had the Force Publique been disarmed when to do so would still have been comparatively easy.

But criticisms about the UN operations – and there is no lack of critics – become insignificant when set, as they should be, against the prophylactic role of the UN. It remains the one strong, firm, encouraging factor in the Congo situation. If it collapses much more than the peace of the Congo would be lost.

LEOPOLDVILLE
1 December 1960

Chapter 1

PROPHET OF DISASTER

'Feel considerably in doubt about the future.'
An entry made in Joseph Conrad's Notebooks
in Matidi, 13 June 1890

THE disaster that twice overtook the Belgians in the Congo – at the turn of the present century, and again in 1960 – cannot be explained only in terms of more recent events. The roots of the Congo's tragedy go deep; they belong, perhaps, more to the past than to the present. 'Time future contained in time past' is the poet's contribution towards understanding social forces. Seventy years ago Joseph Conrad foreshadowed disaster in the Congo. His imagination and insight helped him to understand the tensions of the Congolese as well as of the Belgians, and made it possible for him to penetrate into the reality of King Leopold's Congo.

Conrad had gone to Africa as a young man in 1890, and had learned navigation on the little-known Congo river. He was appalled by what he saw. His impressions, scribbled in pencil in two black penny notebooks, were later woven into his two tales of the Congo – 'An Outpost of Progress' and 'Heart of Darkness'. Of the latter – the more important of the two stories – he wrote: 'It is experience pushed a little (and only a little) beyond the actual facts of the case.'

The Congo of Conrad's day no longer exists; only the memory of it. Unfortunately, memory is not a passive force. If the older generation of British workers still acts under the impulse of unemployment in the 1930s, how much less surprising is it to find suspicions of the past still acting as a powerful factor in the Congo, with its large, isolated peasant communities and their untrained political leaders. The past is often the only measurement they have to guide them in new and unfamiliar situations.

Going up the river Conrad knew and described so well is still like travelling back to the earliest beginnings of the world, when vegetation rioted on the earth and big trees were kings. There is still the vast, ominous stillness that does not in the least resemble a peace. For Conrad 'it was the stillness of an implacable force brooding over an inscrutable intention. It looked at you with a vengeful aspect.' This threat of vengeance was overwhelming. In 'An Outpost of Progress' the two 'agents of civilization', Carlier and Kayerts, finally succumbed to their fear of 'things vague, uncontrollable, and repulsive.' Their outpost disintegrated; they left a village 'mourning for those they had lost by the witchcraft of white men, who had brought wicked people into the country. The wicked people had gone, but fear remained. *Fear always remains.*'

In 'Heart of Darkness' Conrad describes the death of one of the agents of King Leopold's commercial enterprise. Kurtz was a legend among the Company's agents because of his devotion to its interests and his success in collecting ivory. His methods were barbaric; but those who knew the truth dared not speak for fear of offending the Company. Did Conrad have King Leopold in mind when he described the schizophrenic Kurtz? Although students of Conrad seem never to have considered this possibility the evidence for it is strong. The report Kurtz wrote for the imaginary 'International Society for the Suppression of Savage Customs'* begins with the argument that 'we whites, from the point of development we arrived at, must necessarily appear to them [the savages] in the nature of supernatural beings – we approach them with the might of a deity. . . . By the simple exercise of our will we can exercise a power for good practically unbounded.' Commenting on this report Conrad says: 'It gave me the notion of an exotic Immensity ruled by an august Benevolence.'

It is easy to see Leopold, clad in his augustan Benevolence, dedicating himself to the interests of the exotic Immensity of Congolese as he stood before a distinguished international audience in 1876: 'The slave trade, which still exists over a large part of the African continent, is a plague spot that every friend

---

* Compare this title with the 'International Association for the Exploration and Civilization of Central Africa' launched by King Leopold fourteen years before Conrad went to the Congo. Leopold was entrusted by Europe with the task of suppressing slavery and rooting out barbarism.

of civilization would desire to see disappear. The horror of that traffic, the thousands of victims massacred each year . . . the still greater number of perfectly innocent beings who, brutally reduced to captivity, are condemned *en masse* to forced labour . . . makes our epoch blush. . . .'

This was the King who soon afterwards was himself to introduce forced labour on a scale unknown in modern times until the advent of Hitler. Under his rule thousands of victims were to be massacred every year. Until international opinion became so scandalized that it compelled the Belgian nation to act against their King, he made an 'epoch blush' for his crimes. All this still belonged to the future, but Conrad had already got the smell of what was happening. He describes Kurtz's trading post, ringed by poles on each of which was a shrunken head. One of Kurtz's admirers explained: 'These heads were the heads of rebels.' To which Conrad's narrator replies: 'Rebels! What would be the next definition I was to hear? There had been enemies, criminals, workers – and these were rebels. Those rebellious heads looked very subdued to me on their sticks.'

Kurtz's credo, like his royal employer's, was a simple one. 'You show them [the natives] you have in you something that is really profitable, and then there will be no limits to the recognition of your ability. Of course you must take care of the motives – right motives – always.' Kurtz dies screaming: 'The Horror! The Horror!' Leopold, so far as one knows, died more peacefully.

Joseph Conrad was haunted by his closeness to the Congolese. 'You know, that was the worst of it – this suspicion of their not being inhuman. It would come slowly to one. They howled, and leaped, and spun, and made horrible faces; but what thrilled you was just the thought of their humanity – like yours – the thought of your remote kinship with this wild and passionate uproar.'

Chapter 2

RIVALS FOR THE CONGO

'The exploration of Africa had given rise to the desire to absorb it. The old view that Africa was a continent of no value had been shaken, and was on the eve of passing away.'

DEMETRIUS C. BOULGER. *The Congo State*

THE Congo's threat to world peace in 1960 was not the first time it has produced an international crisis. The discovery of the importance of the Congo river, through H. M. Stanley's explorations in 1874, precipitated a crisis that threatened to upset the 'balance of power' in Europe. It led directly to Europe's decision ten years later to draw up rules governing the 'carve-up' of Africa; only in this way was it possible to prevent the nineteenth-century scramble for colonies leading to war.

Stanley had returned from his journey in the Congo with high ambitions for its development. 'This river is, and will be, the grand highway of commerce in West Central Africa,' he wrote in a dispatch to the *Daily Telegraph* in 1876. 'I feel convinced that the question of this mighty waterway will become a political one in time.' It did, though not in the way Stanley had imagined it would. But the moment of his return was unpropitious. Britain was distracted by other problems, and Gladstone's Liberal Administration was in no mood for further involvements in Africa just then. This attitude quickly changed when other nations became interested in Stanley's offer. Although Britain did not want the Congo for herself – the potential wealth of Katanga had not yet been discovered – she wanted to ensure that its control would pass into the right hands; that freedom of commerce would be guaranteed; and that slavery would be vigorously combated. Her favourite for the Congo was Portugal. But France and Germany had other ideas, and the King of the Belgians had ambitions of his own.

Poor Stanley – all his life he had longed for nothing more than to win recognition in his mother country – found his gift of the Congo spurned when he laid it at the feet of Britain. He was widely denounced for his quixoticism. 'In 1878', he wrote, 'that word was flung in my teeth several times especially by Manchester men ... a Manchester editor, or a Manchester merchant, almost invariably taunted me with being a "dreamer", a "quixotic journalist", or a mere "penny-a-liner".'

But if Britain had no use for the 'penny-a-liner' the King of the Belgians did. He had already tried to ensnare the tired explorer at Marseille on his way back to London after his gruelling 999-day trek across Africa. After his rebuff in London and Manchester (where he had hoped to interest the merchants in the commercial possibilities of the great Congo basin) Stanley went to Brussels. There he met with something more than the polite formality with which Queen Victoria had received him.

THE KING TAKES A HAND

Leopold II was a remarkable monarch. He loved pleasure and money with an equally ferocious appetite. He was handsome, with a fine, bold beard; his cynical, worldly charm bore with dignity his other title – the King of Maxim's. But there was much more to Leopold than this life of pleasure-seeking. He had vast ambitions, for himself as well as for his country. Tiny Belgium was too confining for his great energies, and he found the cautious ambitions of his people oppressively restrictive. He soared above and beyond them, like an eagle trying to escape from its gilded cage. In 1860, freshly back from a voyage to the East, he had tried to widen the Belgians' horizons. 'I claim for Belgium her share of the sea.' Stanley's discoveries showed him the way to make good this claim.

In 1876 he summoned a conference in Brussels to which he invited representatives from Europe and America to launch what came to be known as the International African Association. There he spoke as a humanitarian, and as one interested in geographic exploration for the sake of science. 'To open to civilization the only part of the globe where it has not yet penetrated, to pierce the darkness shrouding entire populations, that is, if I may venture to say so, a crusade worthy of this century of progress. . . .' But from beneath his affable altruism there peeped just the hint of a financier presiding over a board meeting. 'Among those who have most closely studied Africa, a good many have been led to think that there would be advantage to the common object they pursued if they could be brought together for the purpose of conference with the object of regulating the march, combining the efforts, deriving some profit from all circumstances, and from all resources, and finally, in order to avoid doing the same work twice over.'

But lest anybody should think the King had any personal ambitions for Belgium he carefully assured the conference: 'No, gentlemen: if Belgium is small, she is happy and satisfied with her lot.'

The game thus set, Leopold began to play his cards with winning skill. He attracted to his royal patronage a large body of distinguished and disinterested explorers, geographers, and diplomats. One of these was the American Ambassador in Brussels at the time, Mr Sanford, who shortly came to play an extraordinary role in getting United States backing for Leopold's venture.

The International African Society spawned a separate venture, the Comité d'Études du Haut Congo, to realize the ambitions of Stanley to build a railway from the point where the cataracts in the Lower Congo make the river unnavigable to a point below the present Leopoldville. The International African Association adopted its own flag, two gold stars on a blue background, and sent Stanley to negotiate treaties with African rulers in the Congo to open the way for peaceful commerce and occupation, and to set in hand arrangements for building the railway line to which Leopold had pledged a part of his own private fortune. With Stanley thus engaged, Leopold developed a Public Relations campaign which would have done credit to modern practitioners of this art. He set to work his distinguished volunteers, whose advocacy was so successful that the Great Powers began to grow restless.

Portugal had always fancied her own pretensions to the Congo, and in 1881 Britain signed a treaty recognizing Portuguese rights to a limited part of the territory. This treaty produced an immediate reaction in both Britain and Germany. The Chambers of

Commerce of Manchester and Glasgow attacked it on the grounds of its restrictions on legitimate trade, and found a champion in the House of Commons in the redoubtable John Bright. The Liverpool African Associates, supported by the Baptist missionary associations, attacked the treaty because they feared the Portuguese would not stamp out slavery, while the cause of Protestantism would be hindered. In Germany, the Chambers of Commerce moved with their counterparts in Britain, and Holland soon followed suit. Meanwhile, France had dispatched de Brazza to the north bank of the Congo to discover suitable points on which to plant the tricolour. By 1882 the European Powers were rapidly moving towards conflict.

At this critical moment two unrelated events developed in Leopold's favour. The President of the United States decided to recognize the validity of the flag of the International African Association, even though it was flown by a purely private commercial association and not by a sovereign state. The spadework for this surprising decision had been skilfully done by Sanford who had resigned as the U.S. Ambassador to Brussels to become associated with Leopold's enterprise. America's decision, 'taken in the interests of commercial freedom', came as a blow to Britain. She found it convenient to disentangle herself from her treaty with Portugal which, in any event, had been rejected by the Cortes.

The second development was the initiative taken by Prince von Bismarck, Chancellor of Germany. His interest was to prevent any of Germany's large European competitors gaining a foothold in the Congo. France, too, was engaged. Neither wished to see Britain, or her ally Portugal, entrenched in the Congo.

Bismarck had no difficulty in persuading France to the idea of a conference in Berlin to settle the future of the Congo on the lines of the decisions of the Vienna Congress on the freedom of navigation on international waterways. This would also enable them to raise the question of the Niger over which Britain had by then largely gained control. Together, Germany and France pressed their invitation on Britain to come to Berlin; Lord Granville equivocated – yes to the conference, no to the inclusion of the Niger. Faced with Granville's careful reluctance, Bismarck turned to the United States, having first extended Germany's recognition to the flag of the International African Association. America at once accepted the idea of the Berlin Conference, leaving Britain with no alternative but to accept too.

EUROPE'S MAGNA CARTA IN AFRICA

The Berlin Conference, which met on 15 November 1884 and continued until 26 February 1885, was one of the landmarks in the relations between Europe and Africa. What had started as an attempt to settle the limited question of the Congo ended up in a general agreement between the European Powers to recognize each other's rights in Africa. This became the Magna Carta of the colonial powers in Africa.

Fourteen nations* came to the conference, including all the principal rivals in the 'scramble for Africa'. The tone was set by Bismarck in his opening address. Experience in the Far East, he said, had shown that the best results could be obtained by 'restraining commerce within legitimate competition'. Regulated commerce in Africa could benefit everybody, but Commerce must be linked to Civilization. 'All the Governments invited here', declared Bismarck, 'share the desire to associate the natives of Africa with civilization, by opening up the interior of that continent to commerce, by furnishing the natives with the means of instruction, by encouraging missions and enterprises so that useful knowledge may be disseminated, and by paving the way to the suppression of slavery, and especially of the slave trade among the blacks. . . .' It was left to the British representative to remind the conference that 'the natives are not represented at this conference, and that, nevertheless, the decision of this body will be of the gravest importance to them.' But Britain was treated with suspicion, and found herself more or less isolated in the company of the Continental Powers. Portugal alone was loyal, within the limits of her own interests. America was committed to a line different from Britain's.

It is remarkable that any agreement should have been possible

* Germany, Austria, Belgium, Denmark, Spain, United States, France, Britain, Italy, Holland, Portugal, Russia, Sweden and Norway, and Turkey.

in this welter of rivalries. By December 1884 it looked as if the conference would end in failure. Britain was determinedly resisting efforts to include her territories on the east coast of Africa and the Niger river in the terms of the agreement; France was pushing her claims for territorial rights on the north bank of the Congo; Portugal was determined to hang on to what she had carved out for herself around the mouth of the Congo; Germany was skilfully manoeuvring the lesser of her rivals against the greater. The Belgian representatives were pushing for recognition of the International African Association as the sovereign owner of clearly defined borders within the Congo, and to render it immune from attack by other powers through recognition of its status as a neutral.

Stanley, called in as a technical adviser to the U.S. delegation (although he was already an employee of the Belgian King), found himself out of his depth in this European wilderness. Everything appeared so simple to him; why all the fuss? 'If the conference breaks up before the question between us [the International African Association] and France is settled we are ruined,' he wrote to tell Mr James F. Hutton in Massachusetts. 'The declaration that we are an independent state only makes the bait more tempting for France on one side, and Portugal on the other. We should be like a moth, only created for one day's sunshine and then oblivion. . . . We do not want war because whoever will win the natives will suffer through the struggle. Why should the natives suffer? What have they done?'

THE ROLE OF AMERICA

One of the many curious aspects of the Berlin conference was the role played in it by the United States. What was she doing there at all? And why should her official representative be associated with two of King Leopold's agents? Mr H. S. Sanford (whom we have already encountered – first as U.S. Ambassador in Brussels and later as an associate of the King of the Belgians) was an active intermediary in the conference, and between Berlin and Washington. Stanley, perplexed, and anxious only to build his railway line in the Congo, played a less important part as a technical adviser. Although America spoke formally through its

Ambassador in Berlin, John A. Kasson, the direction of policy
was firmly in Sanford's hands. The official records of the U.S.
Congress leave no doubt at all on this point. It is an extraordinary
fact that at an international conference of such a nature America's
policy should have been directed largely, if not wholly, by an
American who was the agent of a foreign King.

Not unnaturally, the Senate and Congress showed increasing
interest in the American role at the Berlin Conference. But
although the President was vigorously assailed, his policy of
intervention in Africa was allowed to continue until the final
stage. Having played a prominent part in the negotiations, the
United States declined to sign the final Agreement. It did, however, ratify the Brussels Act of 1890 which was the sequel to the
Berlin Act.

Perry Belmont was one of the Congressmen who vigorously
pursued the President. 'Did not the question of the Congo turn
out at Berlin to be a "European broil"? Was it not from the
beginning obviously such?' Arguing that participation in the
conference was a departure from the Monroe Doctrine of non-
intervention, he charged: 'What was desired or sought, as we now
clearly see, by assembling the Conference at Berlin, was the
persuasion or moral coercion either to recognize or define the
jurisdiction in Africa of the International African Association,
or of France, or of Portugal, or of some other power, or to
reconcile the rivalries and conflicting claims of each and all, in
order that the rights of the aboriginal and uncivilized tribes may
be subordinated or respected; slavery and slave labour be destroyed and prevented; facilities afforded in Africa for Christian
missionaries of all nations and tongues; fair and equal access to
the Congo region and just treatment therein for all traders
provided; a limit to all charges and taxes on foreign trade, and
all offensive monopolies excluded. Certainly all those are bene-
ficent and desirable objects. But at least for us in the United
States they were and are, when to be worked out in Berlin for
Africa, *European* objects.'

America's desire to uphold the principle of freedom of commerce would have been a natural answer to the President's
critics; but her spokesmen at the Berlin Conference, supported
by the State Department, chose to defend their position on much

wider grounds. Mr Kasson's opening statement at the Berlin Conference throws considerable light on the success of the methods developed by Leopold and by his team of distinguished associates.

The American case was hung on Stanley, an American by accident and an Englishman by preference, who, at the end of his life, sat without distinction as a Tory M.P. on the back benches of Westminster. Mr Kasson skilfully deployed Stanley's American citizenship to justify American intervention. 'It is to be observed that from the time he left the eastern coast of Africa opposite Zanzibar, during his travels to and beyond the upper waters of the Nile as far as the watershed of the Congo, and along the entire course of that great river while slowly descending towards the sea, and until he saw an ocean steamer lying in the Lower Congo, he found nowhere the presence of civilized authority, no jurisdiction claimed by any representative of white men save his own over his retainers, no dominant flag or fortress of a civilized power, and no sovereignty exercised or claimed except that of the indigenous tribes. His discoveries aroused the attention of all nations. It was evident that very soon that country would be exposed to the dangerous rivalries of conflicting nationalities. There was even danger of its being so appropriated as to exclude it from free intercourse with a large part of the civilized world. It was the earnest desire of the Government of the United States that these discoveries should be utilized for the civilization of the native races, and for the abolition of the slave trade and that early action should be taken to avoid international conflicts likely to arise from national rivalry in the acquisition of special privileges in the vast region so suddenly exposed to commercial enterprises. If that country could be neutralized against aggression, with equal privileges for all, such an arrangement ought, in the opinion of my Government, to secure general satisfaction.'

In a revealing dispatch to the U.S. Secretary of State on 14 January 1885, Sanford describes how the Berlin Conference was facilitated by America's recognition of the flag of the International African Association of the Congo as that of a friendly government. This recognition, he added, assured the existence of the Association 'menaced by the pretensions and greed of European powers, and secured to the United States (and the world as

well) freedom of commerce and equal rights, and also the abolition of the slave trade in a region of about a million square miles,
the richest portion of Africa.'

He went on to explain: 'With regard to the "objects or purposes" for which our Government is represented at the Conference, I will only speak now of those which "led up" to the
invitation to participate in it. In the first place, an American
citizen, Mr Stanley, had discovered this region, and theoretically
certain rights may be assumed to have inured thereby to the
United States; another citizen (myself) had been engaged from
the very inception of the work, as a member of the executive
committee of the International Association, in building up in this
barbarous region this future state and securing certain rights to
his country therein; and the Government of the United States
had formally recognized its sovereignty, and thereby acquired
rights and privileges for its citizens over a great portion of
Central Africa.'

Speaking of his own role and of his motives he said: 'It does
not become me to speak of my part in the transaction, save to say
that active participation, from its inception, with the African
International Association, had impressed me, as it progressed,
with the importance to our commerce and manufactures, to our
races of African descent,* and to civilization, if this vast region
which the munificence of King Leopold was opening to civilizing
influences could be made free to our merchants and missionaries,
and especially to the enterprise of our coloured citizens. The
dangers, too, to our citizens there engaged in this work, Mr
Stanley and his assistants, who were liable to be treated, in default
of a recognized flag, as pirates, was another reason that *influenced
me in making representations both to the association and to the
President (of the U.S.A.) which resulted in this recognition*'.

THE BERLIN TREATY

In the end the conference achieved a successful compromise. It
guaranteed freedom of trade in the Congo Basin; guaranteed

* Throughout his lobbying Sanford had made a special point of stressing
the interests of American Negroes in the Congo, although he never tried to
define what their interests might be.

freedom of navigation on the Congo river, as well as on the Niger; agreed on militant action against the slave trade; and adopted a declaration introducing into international relations uniform rules about future occupation on the coasts of Africa. This Magna Carta of the colonial powers was the unexpected offshoot of Stanley's exploits in the Congo.

The Declaration lays down with deceptive simplicity that 'any power which henceforth *takes possession* of a tract of land on the coasts of the African continent, outside of its present possessions, *shall acquire it*, as well as the power which assumes a protectorate there, shall accompany the respective act with a notification thereof, addressed to the other signatory powers of the present Act, in order to enable them, if need be, to make good any claims of their own'.

In plain terms this means that any European power which, by treaty or by conquest, picked out a choice bit of Africa's coast would be recognized as its lawful ruler, provided no other power had already laid claims to it.

The conference's decisions provided a framework within which King Leopold could develop a Free State in the Congo. The King had done a magnificent job of selling his ideas; he was greatly helped by the smallness of Belgium which made her a safe buffer between the rivals for the Congo. Bismarck, in particular, took up Leopold's cause. In his concluding address he expressed the prevailing sentiment about 'the noble efforts of His Majesty the King of the Belgians, the founder of a work which is today recognized by all the Powers, and which by its consolidation may render precious service to the cause of humanity'.

Alas for these noble sentiments, the choice by Europe and America of Leopold, as their agent of civilization in Africa, soon turned into shameful disaster.

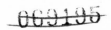

Chapter 3

LEOPOLD'S KINGDOM

> '*The wealth of a sovereign consists in public property; it alone can constitute in his eyes an enviable treasure, which he should endeavour constantly to increase.*'
>
> KING LEOPOLD II

THE Congo Free State was established in 1885. It succeeded the Congo International Association founded in 1883 as an offshoot of the International African Association. Leopold found himself entrusted personally with a domain covering more than 900,000 square miles, almost the size of Europe.

Although the Belgians rejoiced in their King's triumph they were in no mood to claim the Congo as a possession of Belgium. If the King wanted to shoulder the responsibilities, financial and otherwise, he was welcome to do so. All he could expect from the Belgians was their good wishes, coupled with the anticipation that if things went unexpectedly well they would share in the benefits. 'May the Congo, gentlemen, from this day forth, offer to our superabundant activity, to our industries, more and more confined, outlets by which we shall know how to profit,' exclaimed the Minister of Finance in a speech asking the Belgian Chamber to ratify the decisions of Berlin. 'May the enterprising spirit of the King encourage our countrymen to seek, even at a distance, new sources of greatness and prosperity for our dear country.' And the King, in his characteristic reply, underlined his own responsibilities: 'I have confidence in success, and I wish that Belgium, *without it costing her anything*, should find in these vast territories, freed from all tax of admission, new elements of development and prosperity.' But the King had much more difficulty persuading the Belgians of the wisdom of his next proposal: that he should wear two crowns – one for Belgium and the other for the Congo. After a fierce controversy, the Chamber and the Senate decided: 'His Majesty Leopold II, King of the Belgians, is authorized to be chief of the State founded in Africa by the International Association of the Congo. The Union between Belgium and the new State of the Congo shall be *exclusively personal.*'

THE RAVAGED LAND

When Leopold embarked on his 'civilizing mission' in the Congo in 1885, the people were in a pitiable condition. Hunger had contributed towards producing a state of cannibalism on a scale unknown in other parts of the continent. No country had suffered more from slavery. One officially quoted Belgian figure put the total loss at 30 millions, more than twice the present population. At the height of slavery 50,000 men, women, and children were taken annually from the Congo to the New World; the numbers going out by the Arab slave routes were much higher. Tipoo Tip, the King of Arab slavers, was firmly entrenched in the eastern Congo, and his slave raids continued in blissful disregard of the European conventions decreeing its abolition.

Vast areas of the country had become entirely depopulated; insecurity, fear, and suspicion were the rulers, except in remote areas unpenetrated by the slavers and by their African collaborators. Here and there one still came across a tranquil part of the country with glimpses of what life was like when the celebrated art of the Congo craftsmen flourished, and when village life was normal. Leo Frobenius, German explorer and humanist, visited Kasai-Sankuru at the turn of the century. 'In some villages, the main streets were lined on both sides with palm trees. Each hut was adorned in a different style, a clever, delightful mingling of wood-carving and matting. The men carried chiselled weapons in bronze and brass. They were clad in multi-coloured stuffs of silk and fibre. Each object, pipe, spoon, or bowl was a work of art, comparable in its perfect beauty to the creations of the romanesque period in Europe. I have never heard of any northern people who could rival these primitive folk in their dignity, exquisite politeness, and grace.'*

The Congo had never been a political entity; it was a gigantic geographical sprawl from the Atlantic ocean over the vast Congo Basin to the foothills of the Mountains of the Moon.

* *Kulturgeschichte Afrikas*, Zürich, 1933.

Hundreds of tribes, subdivided into a thousand or more clans, survived in more or less suspicious isolation. Few of the powerful tribes of earlier times had survived the depredations of slavery. The once great Kingdom of the Bakongo – the only remarkable nation-state known to have existed in that part of the world – had long before crumbled into decadence. (The attempt to recreate the past greatness of the Bakongo is one of the factors that many years later was to contribute to the downfall of Belgian rule.)

RUM AND CRINGLETS

How does a King in Europe, who has never set eyes on Tropical Africa, set about organizing a modern state there? The starting-point was easy enough; the concept was Stanley's. It was to build a railway line to the sea, providing a continuous line of communications for more than a thousand miles into the interior and to establish trading-posts along the river's entire length. The immediate objective was ivory and rubber. To get the land to establish trading-posts it was necessary to enter into treaties with the chiefs. Stanley quickly signed more than a hundred treaties; their terms were simple, and the rights they conferred not very costly. The treaties provided for absolute cession and abandonment to the Congo International Association of areas of land belonging to chiefs. They surrendered any right to levy tolls, or dispose of the natural resources in their territories; they ceded the right to cultivate unoccupied lands, to exploit the forests, to fell trees, and to gather all natural products; finally, they obliged the chiefs to furnish labour, and to join forces against 'all intruders of no matter what colour'.

The treaty of Palla Balla gives a general idea of the payment made for these rights: one coat of red cloth with gold facing, one red cap, one white tunic, one piece of white caft, one piece of red points, one dozen boxes of liqueurs, four demijohns of rum, two boxes of gin, 128 bottles of gin (Hollands), twenty pieces of red handkerchieves, forty cringlets, and forty red cotton caps.

LORD OF THE FORESTS

Leopold quickly discovered that the enterprise was more costly than even his considerable private fortune could bear. In the early stages of development he had committed £1,200,000 of his own money. He naturally became anxious for larger and quicker returns. One of his first acts in July 1885 was to make himself owner of all the unoccupied lands in the Congo, thus acquiring by a stroke of the pen personal properties the size of Poland. These lands he parcelled out to private concessionaires who were given monopoly rights to the collection of rubber, ivory, palm oil, and other natural products. Later he went further. In a secret decree he laid claims for the State (that is, for himself) to all the natural products on the vacant lands. This meant that the concessionaires were compelled to pay twice: once for their concession, and a second levy for collecting what was on the land. It also deprived the natives of their right to gather natural wealth from the forests, and confined them to their own demarcated lands. These decrees stretched treaties like that of Palla Balla far beyond their original intentions. Naturally, the chiefs and natives cried out against these decisions; but these protests were treated as rebellion, and were forcibly put down.

Still the rewards were not what Leopold had expected or demanded. As the unchallenged sovereign authority he was free to command any changes that might suit his policies and his pocket. One of his great British admirers wrote in 1898,* 'the Congo is governed by a simple and swift-dealing autocracy'. The autocrat decreed that Africans could sell their products only to the King's agents; this was only one short step away from imposing a system of forced labour on the country, which came next. The overriding consideration was more rubber and more ivory; more, at lower prices. Accordingly the price of these products was officially reduced. Again there were protests, and again law and order was imposed.

An order was issued by a high official in the King's employ to all agents of the Company. 'I have the honour to inform you that from 1 January 1899 you must succeed in furnishing four thousand kilos of rubber every month. To effect this I give you *carte blanche*. You have therefore two months in which to work your people. Employ gentleness first, and if they persist in not

* Demetrius C. Boulger. *The Congo State, or the Growth of Civilization in Central Africa*. London, 1898.

accepting the imposition of the state, employ force of arms.' The agents did not have to wait for such explicit orders. Joseph Conrad's Kurtz had operated along these lines long before he had permission to do so. Did Leopold know what was happening in the Congo? His instructions to his agents make it clear that he not only knew, but approved. His attitude (two years before the instructions quoted above was issued) was that civilization could not be bought cheaply. 'Placed in front of primitive savagery . . . they [the Association's agents] have to bring them [the savages] gradually to submission. It is necessary for them to subject the population to new laws, of which the most imperious and the most salutary is assuredly that of labour.'

In a letter addressed to his agents when their methods were being fiercely criticized in 1897, the King reminded them at the same time that the native population was the base of the region's true wealth. But, while that must always be kept in mind, results 'cannot be achieved by words alone, however philanthropic their sound may be.' The King, though opposed to unnecessary force, upheld its use 'in view of the necessary domination by civilization'. He went on: 'Wars that are not indispensable ruin the regions in which they take place. Our agents are not ignorant of this. The day that their effective superiority is established, it will be profoundly repugnant to them to abuse it. . . . Animated by a pure sentiment of patriotism, scarcely sparing their own blood, they [the agents] will be all the more careful of the blood of the natives, who will see in them the all-powerful protectors of their lives and property, the benevolent instructors of whom they have a great need.'

But the flood of international protest was beginning to rise so that even Belgium could no longer stop her ears to the truth of what was being done in her name. The Belgians had had their first shock over Stanley's relations with Tippoo Tip, the Arab slave leader and an old acquaintance with whom he had had previous financial dealings. Leopold had gained considerable support for his enterprise by his dedicated promise to abolish slavery. Yet one of Stanley's first actions was to appoint the leader of the slavers as a governor of the Association. His excuse was that they were not yet ready to face an attack on their young enterprise by the powerful Tippoo Tip. The best thing was to cooperate with him until the time came to destroy him.

Cardinal Lavigerie, the ardent abolitionist, was among the first to arouse the Belgians to the monstrosity of this arrangement. Where was the campaign promised to destroy the slavers? Criticism swelled into public protests in Brussels; and the conscience of the Belgian people found expression in the Congo Reform Association.

When Leopold finally ordered the Force Publique to attack the Arab slavers, it took three years to break their power. A latter-day Belgian historian* suggests that the King's campaign against Tippoo Tip was not wholly inspired by anti-slavery sentiments, but had a great deal to do with the economic threat of the Arab traders to his monopoly system in the Congo.

BRITAIN TAKES A HAND

The methods authorized and vigorously defended by King Leopold grew to be an international scandal. In Belgium, the Socialist leader, Émile van der Velde, and Catholic journalists, led the attack on their King. German and American missionaries reported misdeeds they had witnessed. But it was in Britain that the protest was greatest. The Congo Reform Association – under the scourging leadership of E. D. Morel, the author of *Red Rubber* which exposed Leopold's methods – led the nation to protest. In 1903 the House of Commons agreed, without a division, to consult with the signatories of the Berlin Treaty 'that measures may be taken to abate the evils in that state [the Congo Free State]'.

A British White Paper, based largely on the reports of Roger Casement and of other British consuls in the Congo, documented the horrors in the Congo. Vice-consul Mitchell, reporting in 1906, wrote: 'I am not aware of any civilized State in which conscription is applied to "works of public utility" . . . Those "paid workmen" are the conscripts! They are hunted in the forests by soldiers, and are brought in bound by the neck like criminals.' Another consul, W. G. Thesiger, wrote two years later: 'There

* R. P. P. Ceulemans: *La Question arabe et le Congo* (*1883–1892*). Brussels, 1960.

are continual police raids carried on [in the Ituri district] with the greatest energy, in which native villages are destroyed and such prisoners as can be taken sent in chains to work on the *Railway des Grands Lacs.*'

In a book* describing conditions in fifteen rubber and copal factories, a German doctor, W. Doerpinghaus, wrote of 'a well-organized system of compulsory labour, for the maintenance of which the agents employ, with the tacit toleration of the management, every means which brutality and coarseness have ever invented. . . . The history of modern civilized nations has scarcely ever had anything to equal such shameful deeds as the agents in the Belgian Congo have rendered themselves guilty of. That the Company is aware of the doings of its agents, tolerates them, and encourages them, I can produce flagrant proof . . . I must add that the natives of the region in question are harmless, and only rise to attack when driven to extremities. I frequently travelled for days without escort. There is therefore not the slightest excuse for the murders and atrocities. . . .'

Official reports to the British Foreign Office, supported with photographic evidence, confirmed the practice of Leopold's agents in cutting off the hand or foot of a labourer who did not fulfil his quotas. Nor are official Belgian sources lacking in details of the measures taken to compel the increasingly rebellious population to work for Leopold's enterprises. The assistant of the Attorney-General in Stanleyville, writing to his chief in 1905, said: 'If these works [the railways] are to be executed, arbitrary measures must be resorted to. The men are taken by force and brought to the works, where they are kept, under fear of the lash and prison.' But he was writing not in protest but to secure legal sanction for these methods.

Decrees authorizing the forcible recruiting of labourers were issued under the general Conscript Law. Article 6 provided for labourers to be subject to military discipline and punishment. This included the 'chain gang', and flogging from four to fifty lashes; the flogging, however, not to exceed twenty-five strokes a day. The British Foreign Secretary, Lord Lansdowne, described this system as 'bondage under the most barbarous and inhuman conditions, and maintained for mercenary motives of the most

* *Deutschlands Rechte und Pflichten gegenüber dem belgischen Kongo.*

selfish character'. British official and unofficial opinion joined together in demanding that the Belgian Government should relieve their King of his 'exclusively personal' rule over the Congo.

'But,' Morel wrote in 1909, 'the Congo enterprise remained throughout personal and not national in complexion. Sections of the upper and middle class secured handsome returns; contractors did a flourishing business for a time; much wealth accrued to Antwerp in particular. Never was wealth so demonstrably the produce of systematized evil-doing. There were none of the intermediate stages which confuse issues and defy detection by the difficulty of tracing cause and effect. In this case cause and effect were separated only by the extortion of the raw material from the natives accompanied by wholesale massacre and by every species of bestial outrage which diseased minds could invent, the unloading of that raw material upon the Antwerp quays, and the disposal of it on the market. . . . The Belgian people thus became *de facto* although not *de jure* identified with a system of colonial government recalling, but surpassing, the worst example of medieval history. To a people wholly ignorant of the problems incidental to the government of coloured races, the African was represented as a brute beast with no rights in his soil, in his labour, or in his person. And this pestilent doctrine was popularized by a mechanism of financial, political, and Press corruption which for comprehensiveness has seldom been equalled, and which bit deep into the national life of Belgium. It was a double wrong; upon the people of the Congo, and upon the people of Belgium.'*

The United States and Turkey, alone among all the nations who had been present at the Berlin conference, sided with Britain in demanding action from the Belgian Parliament. But the international campaign of the Congo Reform Association, together with the rising criticisms inside Belgium, and a series of revolts in the Congo, compelled the King to hold an official inquiry into the affairs of the Congo in 1904. Two years later its findings were published confirming the existence of widespread abuses, and making proposals for reforms. It also recorded its 'admiration for the signs of advancing civilization' which it had observed.

* E. D. Morel. *Africa and the Peace of Europe*. London, 1909.

Finally, the Belgians were compelled to act against their King. He now began to bargain with his parliament over the terms under which he would relinquish his private Kingdom. He wished to retain as his own domain an area of 155 square miles in Africa, a life interest in property on the Riviera, owned by the Fondation de la Couronne, a villa at Ostend, land at Laeken, a £2 million payment, which he undertook to use for the benefit of the Congo, and annuities to members of the Royal Family. The Belgian Parliament, reluctant to burden itself with this Congo, was unwilling to accept the conditions imposed by Leopold. In the end these terms were rejected, and, after a four-month debate, the Belgian Parliament took over the Congo from their King on 20 August 1908.

But all was not yet well. Belgium at first showed considerable timidity in making a clean break with the past. She continued to operate the Conscript Law as in the days of Leopold. A year after the new dispensation, the Rev. W. M. Morrison of the American Mission in Kasai wrote to the London *Times* giving an eye-witness account of the system that had been denounced by Earl Grey as 'veiled slavery': 'During the month of June a raid was made near Luebo by a State officer. Men and women, boys and girls were taken by force; villages were pillaged; two were burnt; women were raped; chiefs tied up and taken away. . . . Now, the question is, how long will all this keep up? How long can the native races stand this drain? I am sorry to say that so far I can see no material change in the situation under the so-called Belgian regime.'

Morel was back on the warpath with the Congo Reform Association demanding from Britain and America that the Belgian action of annexation should not be recognized until civilized laws had replaced those of Leopold's system. It was not until 1913 that the Congo Reform Association felt satisfied that its main work was accomplished, and that it could wind up its affairs.

THE KING'S LEGACY

It is impossible to say what profits came to Leopold from his Kingdom in the Congo. By 1908 the stock value of his personal estate stood at something like 60 million Belgian francs; but this left out of account his interests in the other companies he had established with the concessionaires. He was ruthless, rapacious, and relentless; there is little one can say in his favour. The Congo was a pitiful land when he took it over; it was more pitiful when he had done with it. Although slavery had finally been put down, forced labour, autocracy, and harsher poverty were put in its place. Roger Casement estimated that the Congo's population had declined by three million under Leopold's regime. If the Congolese no longer hid themselves out of sight of the slavers, they now hid out of fear of the Company's agents. Nearly twenty years later Unilever's representative, L. H. Moseley, reported that several districts he had visited were deserted. Although the population near Lusanga was plentiful they 'prefer for safety to keep away from the *highways of the white man* until sure of security'.

Here was his worst crime; Leopold had replaced the natives' fear of the slaver with a fear of the white man. It is one of the embedded roots in the Congo's disaster. It would be convenient to ignore it, and to pretend that, with the passing of Leopold, his terrible errors passed with him. And indeed Leopold's admirers persist to this day.

POSTCRIPT, 1960

Addressing the Congolese delegates at the conclusion of the Round Table Conference, where they had gained their independence, in February 1960, King Baudouin said: 'More than ever, our thoughts return to King Leopold II, who founded the Congo State some eighty years ago. . . . An exceptional and admirable factor is that my great-great-uncle did not achieve this union through conquest, but essentially by peaceful methods, through a series of treaties signed by the King and the tribal chieftains. Thanks to these treaties, the Belgians were able to establish safety, peace, and all the other prerequisites of prosperity in the heart of Central Africa.'

And a few months later the Belgian Prime Minister, M. Gaston Eyskens, opening the Economic Round Table conference in Brussels, declared: 'You must understand that Belgium has taken to heart the task which was undertaken by our King, Leopold II, and pursued for more than eighty years – against considerable odds – through the work and the courage of a great many of our people. We want to believe that you will not imperil this work, and that you will consider it to be one of the bases of your progress as a free nation.'

Chapter 4

'BLUE CHIP' COLONY

*'Is there a finer relationship than that which exists
between father and child?'*
M. PIERRE WIGNY, Belgian Foreign Minister

No enterprise in Africa was more heavily praised or more confidently pursued than the Belgian development of the Congo. It
is not many years since a British Colonial Secretary (Lord Chan-
dos) paused to wonder if the Belgians had not perhaps produced
the key to successful colonial policy. Even the usually critical
Americans mostly withheld their censure. The Congo was the
'blue chip' colony.

Its disaster, so little expected and seldom foretold, produced
the incomprehension usually reserved for the news of the failure
of an old and safe partnership in the City. It is impossible to
believe that the solid burghers of Brussels have been guilty of a
gigantic fraud. Nor, indeed, have they – unless it is a fraud to
delude themselves. For the Belgians, like almost everybody else,
were completely taken in by *Inforcongo*, perhaps the most
brilliant – and in some ways the most intelligent – propaganda
machine ever created. This Information Service of the Congo
encouraged the Belgians to believe – and they honestly, if un-
critically, did believe – that their colonization of the Congo was
a cause for national pride, and that the Africans loved and
honoured them for their civilizing mission. Nobody knows how
much was spent on *Inforcongo*. It must have been considerable.
But its success was not because of the money spent on it. It had
a good story to tell, of solid economic achievement and of steady
social development. It had a consistent policy in which it believed
– benevolent paternalism. Its tone was positive, unfailingly
courteous, severely practical and high-minded, like the man who
inspired it, Pierre Ryckmans, for long the Congo's almost
legendary Governor-General. 'Rule in order to serve ... this is
the sole excuse for conquest. It is also its complete justification.'

Ryckmans was a stern and just patriarch. Service in the Congo was his life-work, as it was to his son, whose liberal administration won him respect and friendship. When the Belgians hurriedly evacuated Thysville early in August 1960, young Ryckmans returned because he felt his place was with the people he was called upon to serve. They took him prisoner, and a few days later they shot him.

The Belgians were never so aware of their empire as at the moment of losing it. They tried to repudiate it when the Congo fell into their lap; they largely ignored it when they had it, leaving its affairs in the hands of a small coterie of special interests; and they lost it in the end because there was no informed opinion, other than that produced by *Inforcongo*. The Belgians stolidly relied on the men-at-the-top and the men-on-the-spot. In the seventy-five years of their association with the Congo they roused themselves perhaps three or four times on critical aspects of policy.

THE NOBLE IDEA

The law of 18 October 1908, by which Belgium finally assumed control over the Congo, laid down that the interests of the African population were to have absolute priority. The Congo Administration was given a considerable autonomy. Complete separation was established between the finances of Belgium and the Congo. The spirit of the new relationship was that everything had to be done *by* the fortunate Belgians *for* the unfortunate Congolese. In his pastoral letter Cardinal Mercier pointedly expressed the terms of the relationship: 'We should look on colonization as a collective act of charity which, in some circumstances, highly developed nations have to extend to less fortunate races.' That was the attitude in 1908; fifty years later it was precisely the same.

In 1958, M. Pierre Wigny, a former Minister of Colonies and now Foreign Minister, wrote: 'The traditional policy followed by Belgium could be summed up in the word "paternalism". This word is discredited nowadays. Nevertheless, it still connotes a noble idea ... When the Belgians came into Africa the natives had to be taught everything. They knew nothing of writing or building ... They had no idea of what a nation was, or a state, or

even a slightly developed political organization. They had literally to learn to work . . .'*

The new Government of the Congo was a complete bureau-
cracy run by a Governor-General, the virtual ruler of the country;
such limitations as were set to his powers were reserved for the
final authority of the King of the Belgians and of the Belgian
Government. Later he was assisted by purely nominated advisory
councillors; at first only whites, but later blacks as well. Until
1957, when a limited form of local government was introduced,
there were no elections of any kind – a restriction imposed equally
on whites and blacks.

The Administration, too, was a purely Belgian affair; at the
time of independence only one African had risen to a high
position in the civil service – M. Jean Bolikango. He was one of
the senior officers in *Inforcongo*, where it was useful to have
a prominent black propagandist. (Later he was to make a
bitter denunciation of the role he was expected to play in
this propaganda work.) Africanization, which was a feature
of British and French colonialism, was not dreamed of in the
Congo.

The Belgian view was that what the African needed was work,
money in his pocket, food in his belly, education, religion, welfare and health services, peasant agricultural reforms, and technical training. Until 1956 very few Belgians of standing thought
of challenging this concept of the welfare state in the Congo. The
muddles and nasty messes into which British and French colonial
policies periodically landed themselves were smugly cited as
proof of the invincibility of the Belgian method. 'The Congo is
preoccupied above all with practical ends, and is suspicious of the
abstract ideologies which elsewhere in Africa have produced
disastrous results.'†

There was pride in Belgian achievement; and the achievement

* M. Wigny apparently overlooked the Bakongo Kingdom. The intricate
nature of the political organizations of tribes like the Bakongo and the
Lunda, though admittedly not modern, hardly show a lack of knowledge of
social mechanism and organization. As for work, true the Congolese had
to learn to work in a white economy; but their craftsmanship which fills the
Royal Palace at Tervuren in Belgium was not achieved without some effort
or knowledge of the use of tools.

† Ivan Denis. The Belgian Congo. Brussels, 1959.

was a proud one. *Inforcongo* flooded the Congo, Belgium, and the world with glossy accounts of its practical contribution towards uplifting the African. Gross national production rose from £240 million in 1950 to £400 million in 1955; native contribution to the national production rose from 46 per cent of the national income in 1950 to 53 per cent in 1955; the primary schools taught half the child population; nearly 1,400 merchant ships ploughed through some 8,700 miles of navigable waterways; more than 9,000 freight-cars travelled over more than 3,107 miles of railroads, not to mention 800,000 bicycles, nearly 60,000 motor vehicles (with the use of 87,000 miles of roads); 40 airports centralized 20,500 miles of internal airways; the index of sleeping-sickness contamination dropped from 1·2 per cent in 1930 to 0·025 per cent in 1957; over 2,700 hospital units were staffed by 8,000 personnel; the increase in population rose from 6·5 per cent to 12·8 per cent between 1931 and 1953; native consumption – an important sign of widening prosperity – rose from an index of 100 in 1950 to 176 in 1957.

The Belgians had high ambitions for even greater economic development. Their sights were fixed on creating an African equivalent of the Ruhr in the Lower Congo. Only twenty-five miles from the estuary port of Matadi on the Atlantic, the river forms a loop round the Inga plateau. It drops more than a hundred metres in a series of rapids over a distance of only ten miles, and has a flow of 40,000 cubic metres per second, four times greater than Niagara's. When harnessed the river could produce 30 million kilowatts, equivalent to one-fifth of the total electricity capacity of the United States, and three times that of Britain. More important, the cost of electricity would be much lower than the world's lowest price achieved by the Tennessee Valley Authority. The development of this vast cheap hydroelectric energy in a country so richly endowed with raw materials would transform not only the Congo but a large part of the continent as well. The Belgians recognized that they could not develop this African Ruhr from their own resources, and were planning an international effort to bring the Inga project to fruition. Preparatory work was started in 1958 on the first stage, which was expected to take eight years and to cost nearly £110 million.

Who would deny the importance of these achievements? They stand as a monument to the contribution of Belgian skill and enterprise in Africa. What this impressive superstructure lacked, however, was a foundation on which to rest. The Belgian view had always been that economic development and education are the foundation for political independence. It is a popular view, shared by the present rulers of Central Africa and South Africa. But it is a false belief; no enterprise – economic, educational, or religious – can stand unless it is embedded in solid political foundations, which imply government by consent. On this crucial point Belgian policy (like that of the Portuguese) differed from British and French practice in Africa.

THE KATANGA SCANDAL

The Congo's history as a modern economic state begins with the opening up of the mining wealth of the Katanga province in 1911; before that time the emphasis had been on the trade provided by the wealth of the plantations. The discovery of Katanga's wealth completely changed the attitude of the Belgians to their unwelcome colony.

Katanga seems to have been born to controversy; its modern story begins with conflict and bloodshed. Until 1890 this vast south-eastern province of the Congo, the size of Britain, was ruled with great effectiveness and political skill by its King, M'Siri. He was feared by the slavers. He traded with the Arabs in the east and with the Portuguese in the west. Although always anxious to extend his trade, he resisted efforts by white explorers and geologists to stay in his territory. Only one white man, the Scottish missionary Arnot, won his favour. In the end M'Siri was destroyed by the rivalry of two of the shrewdest financiers in Africa's history – Cecil Rhodes and Leopold II.

Although Katanga fell within the territorial limits set by the Berlin conference, Rhodes was not to be easily deterred. Having planted the flag of his Company in Northern Rhodesia he was anxious to lay his hands on the reputed mineral wealth of Katanga. To forestall him, Leopold first floated the Katanga Company, and then dispatched four expeditions to subdue M'Siri. Shortly before he was killed M'Siri sent a message to Cecil Rhodes to come and negotiate a treaty with him; but the messenger mistakenly delivered his note to one of Leopold's agents. Seventy years later history almost repeated itself when agents of Katanga sought the intervention of the latter-day Rhodes, Sir Roy Welensky, with a similar appeal for treaty relationship; but the Belgians forestalled this move too.

Alas for Leopold, it was not until after his death that the true riches of Katanga were revealed. It was called a 'geological scandal' because of the variety and quantity of minerals buried in the relatively small area. This 'scandalously' rich province produces something like 8 per cent of the world's copper, 60 per cent of the West's uranium, 73 per cent of the world's cobalt, 80 per cent of its industrial diamonds, as well as important quantities of gold, zinc, cadmium, manganese, columbium, and tantulum. Its mineral resources appear inexhaustible. Although Katanga holds only 12 per cent of the total population, it contributes 60 per cent of the Congo revenue. It is the economic heart of the country; without it the Congo would be as miserably poor as any of its neighbours. It is obviously worth holding on to.

Katanga's mining wealth is produced by large monopoly companies such as the Union Minière du Haut Katanga (mainly copper and uranium) and Forminière (diamonds). The Union Minière's stock value stood as high as £700 million before the troubles came to the Congo. It contributed almost half of all the country's taxes. But the Union Minière is not entirely its own master. It forms part of the gigantic complex of financial companies erected by the Belgians in the Congo.

The Belgian financial empire formed a State within a State, both within Belgium and within the Congo. It is as though Wall Street or the City of London could, almost at will, wag the tail of the Capitol or of Westminster. In this empire of giants, the biggest is the Société Générale de Belgique; its finger is to be found in most profitable pies – banks, industry, cotton, sugar, pharmacy, motor-cars, beer, railroads, insurance, and Sabena airways. It controls the Compagnie Congolèse du Commerce et de l'Industrie which in its turn controls the Comité Spécial du Katanga (C.S.K.). Remarkably enough it was C.S.K. which granted all mining concessions until independence – a function which in every other country is the prerogative of a Government Department. Two-thirds of the shares of C.S.K. are owned by the Belgian Government, and C.S.K. itself owned 25 per cent of the fabulous Union Minière; the rest was owned by Belgian, British, and American shareholders. C.S.K. has now been wound up; its quarter holding of the Union Minière is being distributed in roughly the proportion of 19 per cent to the Société Générale, 20·5 per cent to British and American interests, and 22·5 per cent to the Congo Government.

The other four monopolies are the Société de Bruxelles pour la Finance et l'Industrie, which also controls the Banque de Bruxelles; the Société Commerciale et Minière du Congo; Huilever, a subsidiary of Unilever; and the Banque Empain.

THE TRINITY OF POWER

Although the Belgian Parliament assumed final responsibility for the affairs of the Congo, it seldom intervened – at least not until after the Second World War. Constitutionally power devolved on the Governor-General but in practice the Congo was ruled by a trinity – the Administration, Big Business, and the Church.

The Roman Catholic Church exerted a predominant influence in the social and educational life of the Congo. In religion as in finance, the monopoly idea was in high favour. Since all education was in the hands of the missions until 1946, you either accepted a Christian education or had nothing. Even the choice of religions was made difficult, because the Catholics enjoyed a twenty-year monopoly of all education subsidies from the State from 1925.

The trinity was in basic agreement on education. Its priority was to concentrate on primary education. More than 1,300,000 children a year went to primary schools. Secondary education came only much later, and in small quantities. As against about a million children in Catholic primary schools, there were fewer than 5,000 in secondary schools, and only slightly more – about 6,000 – in vocational training schools.

If the intention was not to keep the native back, its purpose was to allow him to develop at what the Belgians adjudged to be 'his own pace' There was no question of higher education. The first two university colleges were established in the Congo only in 1956. But although there were no local universities, the trinity's policy was that no Congolese students should go overseas for further studies; a few were allowed to go to the safe seminaries of Rome. The Congo was taken into the first half of the twentieth century tied to a policy that kept all but an inconsiderable fraction of its people to a knowledge of the three Rs and to vocational training. 'In short,' a Belgian apologist wrote,* 'education of the natives is being pushed as fast in the Congo as funds, the native's ability to absorb, *and a care not to upset a delicate social balance by going too fast, will allow.*'

Not too fast! That, in time, was to become the epitaph of the Belgian rule in Africa; the guiding, restraining, parental hand on the shoulder of the child: 'Not too fast, son.'

As late as 1958 Belgian authorities were saying: '*At the end of thirty years* the Belgian system will also produce an *élite* with university training, but unlike the French colonies, the Belgian Congo will have a broad base of literate persons for them to lead.'† In 1960, this was to be but poor consolation for those called upon to lead the first independent government; there were then *less than twelve graduates in the whole of the Congo.*

THE RACE FACTOR

Belgian law in the Congo guaranteed equality between the races; race discrimination was punishable; the colour bar was proscribed. But there was no social equality; segregation was the rule, not the exception; discrimination was practised officially, and its practice was always defended on moral principles. Nevertheless the Belgians denied the existence of racial practices. Just how wide a discrepancy there was between this denial and the reality was savagely exposed by a Belgian Parliamentary Commission that came to the Congo after the start of the troubles in 1959.

Racial discrimination was implicit in the official policy of paternalism; it postulated the doctrine of superiors and inferiors. Superior equalled white; inferior equalled black. This equation

* Eric Cypres.
† *ibid.*

in square one conditioned all race attitudes. The Belgians tried to change the equation by adopting a merit system; an inferior who had achieved certain distinctions in education, religion, employment, or public service could qualify for the status of a superior. He was called an *évolué*; one who had evolved towards being a civilized person. The *évolué* was entitled to all the privileges of the whites, who qualified automatically. The system by which this integration was to take place was called *immatriculation*; the absorption of blacks into the society of the *élite*. The only trouble with this system was that it wouldn't work. The majority of the 100,000 whites in the Congo refused to absorb the *évolués*; and most of the *évolués* did not, in any case, wish to be absorbed. It was a stubborn deadlock that broke the hearts of many sincere authorities. But it never discouraged the young King Baudouin in his patient efforts to shame the whites and to inspire the blacks. He ostentatiously shook hands with Congolese in public, a thing that was seldom done, except by missionaries. He became the godfather of a black baby. Yet at the same time he never missed an opportunity to recall the inspiring leadership of his great-great-uncle, Leopold II.

As in South Africa, Central Africa, and Kenya, blacks and whites lived apart in their own townships; the one community in small houses and huts, the other in large comfortable homes set in large gardens, or in dazzling modern flats. They went to school in separate schools. Desegregated education was given a tentative try-out in 1946; it didn't get very far. Another effort was made in 1957. 'The aim is that the schools should generate the atmosphere of mutual comprehension which will become the solid base on which the inter-racial society of the Belgian Congo will grow.'

The whites, obviously, had all the good jobs; but even on the lower rungs the difference between wages was enormous. Although measures were taken to outlaw the colour bar in ships, trains, places of entertainment, and hotels, the impact remained slight. The majority of the *colons* treated the Africans, *évolués* or otherwise, as inferiors. This was particularly marked in relations between the *petit blancs* and the Congolese in their places of work. It was a source of constant embarrassment and concern to the top Administration and to the Church leadership; their concern was fully justified by what has since happened. The majority of the *petit blancs* were Flemings; they suffered worst in the riots of 1959, and again when the Force Publique ran amok in August 1960. 'Are you a Fleming?' became a general cry among the rebellious soldiers and their camp-followers.

Chapter 5

THE REVOLT OF THE ÉLITE

' Despite the phenomenon of only one European for
140 Africans, the white man has always led the pace
of the Congo's evolution in all its aspects. From the
start, he has dominated the native masses. His
material, cultural, and moral superiority enabled
him to impose his will on the native population with-
out much difficulty. But with the growth of the local
élite, he has lost some of the prestige, which was
based on factors of racial supremacy. This is a
natural and logical phenomenon.'

INFORCONGO, 1958

IN the twelve brief years between 1946 and 1958 the Belgians began to lose what had appeared to be an impregnable position. At any time during that period it had still been possible for them to take the initiative to reverse the drift to defeat; but they ignored the warnings from their own camp, and indignantly repudiated the 'interference' of outsiders like Mr Chester Bowles, a former U.S. Ambassador, who had written with great prescience in 1955: 'The danger lies not so much in the possibility that the Belgians will not compromise eventually with the force of nationalism, but that when they do they will find the Africans almost totally inexperienced in handling the responsibilities which they are certain to demand and eventually to get.'

Three important changes occurred in those twelve years: the break-up of the trinity, the Establishment on which power rested in the Congo; a change of political direction in Brussels; mounting international pressures, responding to developments in other parts of Africa. These pressures found expression in a revolt of the *élite* which led to the final crisis in 1959.

Long before the avalanche hit them, the Belgians had begun to recognize the need to take account of increasing pressures from other parts of Africa, as well as from their own missionary-trained *évolués*, the emancipated, Westernized middle-class. But they completely misjudged the speed of events, and the extent to which it was necessary to make concessions.

Decisions taken in Brussels were blocked in Leopoldville; and decisions taken in Leopoldville were resisted by the *colons*. Looking back over the twelve years after the end of the war, a Belgian parliamentary commission found that the Congo authorities had been tardy and lacking in decision; they also discovered serious weaknesses in the Administration. The efficient machine had begun to run down under the pressure of trying to tailor paternalism to the cut of nationalism.

Until the election of a Liberal-Socialist, in the place of a Catholic, Government in Belgium in 1954, the Establishment in the Congo could rely on getting its own way. But this pattern then began to change; there was a direct conflict between the two Governments over mission education, and particularly with the Catholics. The new Colonial Minister, M. Buissert, was a hustler, impatient of religious monopolies. Having appointed a commission to examine education in the Congo, he was determined to implement their recommendations, which had been severely critical of Catholic methods. They had proposed an extension of lay schools (the few which were started in 1946 had proved extremely popular), as well as drastic cuts in subsidies to mission education. These new policies produced a bitter religio-political conflict in Belgium and the Congo, into which the *évolués* were dragged, first by the Church and later by the secularists. The *évolués* responded eagerly to this appeal for their support. They found themselves in an entirely new situation. Nobody had thought of canvassing their support before this issue came up. Large numbers sided with the Colonial Secretary who suddenly found himself something of a popular hero among the Congolese. This, too, was new. The export of Belgian party divisions to the Congo was severely deprecated by the Governor-General, but joyfully hailed by the *évolués*. It provided them with an opportunity to express veiled nationalist sentiments in terms of anti-clericalism. These developments properly alarmed the Catholic hierarchy.

Elsewhere in Africa, Catholics had already begun to harmonize the Church with the new nationalist forces. A number of Jesuits and liberal Catholics had been pressing for similar changes in the

Congo. This tendency rapidly gained ground after 1954; within two years Catholic presses in the Congo were beginning to publish nationalist tracts. The break-up of the trinity in effect destroyed the *status quo*.

Big Business, too had begun to re-evaluate its role; partly in response to the experiences of the big mining companies in the Central African Federation, and partly in the light of the experience of large companies in those African countries that had gained their independence with the consent of the colonial powers. Though they were by no means agreed, an influential section of Big Business favoured a liberal approach. The small businessmen in the Congo continued, like the *colons* in Algeria, to put their undivided faith in strong government.

THE UNSAFE MIDDLE CLASS

The creation of an African middle class was a central feature of Belgian policy; an *élite* of *évolués*, it was believed, would become the ally of the rulers in maintaining stability and in pursuing reforms in a slow and orderly fashion. This respectable idea was not peculiar to the Belgians. It has long been in the forefront of the thinking of Lord Malvern and Sir Roy Welensky in Central Africa, and of Michael Blundell in Kenya. It says something for their political intelligence that the Afrikaner nationalists in South Africa were never deluded by such ideas. The concept of a solid African middle class, with its bourgeois vested interests in the *status quo*, is clearly not without its attractions. Its weakness lies in the failure to learn from history that revolutions are not made by hungry peasants and by slum-dwellers but by the middle classes and the skilled workers. All African and Asian nationalist movements are led by middle-class elements; this development finally occurred in the Congo too.

The revolt of the *élite* began in an obscure fashion through the formation of what might be likened to old boys' clubs. Because political associations were prohibited in the Congo, the educated Congolese invariably turned to ADAPES (Association des Anciens Élèves des Pères de Scheut) which had been formed with official approval in 1925. Its activities were decently demure and unexciting until after the Second World War, when its membership significantly shot up to 15,000. Its activities, too, were widened to include study circles.

At the same time the number and size of old boys' associations such as Marist Brothers (UNELMA), the Christian Schools (ASANEF), and the schools of the Jesuit Fathers, increased. These associations formed circles of the *évolués* which spread down to small villages. The Belgian authorities and the Church looked with pride on these developments.

Gradually, the tidily-dressed and ambitious clerks and other salary-earners in the Administration and in commerce formed themselves into a nation-wide association of employees, APIC (Association du Personnel Indigène du Congo Belge et du Ruanda-Urundi). This harmless-looking body was formed in 1946. It offered a forum for employees to talk about their wages and conditions, their lack of opportunities, and their experiences at the hands of unsympathetic white supervisors – discussions that led on to questions of ideology such as equal pay for equal work, and the colour bar. The names of practically all the present Congolese leaders appear as officers in these 'harmless' associations.

The Socialists also began to launch study groups, while the Christian leaders sponsored circles devoted to the study of 'social questions'. The best-known of these was UNISCO (Union des Intérêts Sociaux Congolais), whose members were mainly secondary-school pupils. Their first chairman was the highly respectable senior clerk of the Governor-General. Among the most prominent officers of UNISCO and ADAPES was Joseph Kasavubu, then a treasury official, later to become the first President of the Congo Republic. His militant tribal and nationalist consciousness was revealed in one of his earliest addresses to UNISCO in 1946 – equal pay for equal work, Congolese association with the Administration, an urban charter, abolition of the colour bar in all public places. Equally symptomatic of his thinking was his demand of 'Congo for the Congolese', and of the 'Lower Congo for the Bakongo'. This latter demand foreshadowed the formation of the Abako party nearly ten years later.

The formation of tribal associations was the third stage in the development of the Congolese political movement. It flowed directly from the old boys' associations, the employees', Christian, and socialist associations. As in South Africa, the Belgian authorities fostered tribal development in the rural areas, which was carried over when tribesmen came into the urban centres. The Lower Congo – with Leopoldville as its throbbing capital – lies in the Bakongo territory. The Bakongo did not take easily to Belgian rule. They were, at first, slow to send their children to schools; they were against Christianity, and in reaction had created their own tribal religio-political movement which later grew into the Kibanguism* which caused the authorities great trouble until it was finally put down with great severity.

Unlike the Bakongo, the Bangala tribes from the Upper Congo took quickly to Western association. They established themselves in force in Leopoldville; by the time the Bakongo arrived as urban dwellers, the élite of Leopoldville were largely Bangala who greatly outnumbered the Bakongo. The Bakongo reacted by creating the Abako party, to re-assert their influence in the Lower Congo. This naturally produced tribal rivalry. Under Kasavubu's dynamic leadership, Abako forged rapidly ahead. Progress for the Liboke-lya Bangala was much more difficult; they were divided into eight separate tribal units, and they lacked the powerful negative, emotional factors to act as a spur.

In 1957, when the Belgians introduced a limited experiment in democratic elections for the major urban councils, the Bakongo's unity and superior organization enabled them to flatten the Bangala in Leopoldville, securing 62 per cent of the total vote. Thus Kasavubu became the mayor of Dendale in Leopoldville, a platform he used with great skill and determination to champion the cause of Abako.

WIND OF CHANGE

But the turning-point in the Congo came well before 1957. The period between 1946 and 1950 had produced the fabric of social and political organizations; between 1950 and 1955 the circles of the élite began to voice demands for social, economic, and political reforms. During this decade the Congolese were slowly asserting their right to express political opinions. By early 1955 the Congo was beginning to show signs of discomfort. The

* See page 69.

évolués – uneasily poised between the white society and their own illiterates – were pushing with more tenacity and less caution towards open political activities; the *colons* were becoming increasingly critical of their voicelessness in the Congo; the Belgian authorities were trying to find a new system to meet these changing social relationships.

The Governor-General, M. Petillon, publicly aired his views about the need for 'decolonization'. But what did it mean? The Belgians set up a study group to plan the next stage. Typically, they selected only Belgians, and they made their study in Brussels. In the end events overtook their deliberations. Meanwhile, support had grown for the concept of a Belgo-Congolese Community. It envisaged the permanent association of the Congolese with the Belgians: equal members within a single community. Just as the Flemings and the Walloons had joined together, so, too, the Congolese must be integrated into a wider community. In this way the Congo would find its eventual independence within the wider Belgo-Congolese Community. In its essence the idea bears a strong similarity to the French policy for Algeria. Its distinguishing feature is that while the French insist that the Algerians *are* French, the Belgians recognize the separateness of the Congolese.

There was no lack of ideas, or even of new thinking. The air was thick with promises of change. *Inforcongo* blazed away about the great new future that was opening up; it spoke as if decisions about this future had already been taken. But this was precisely what was lacking. There was a political vacuum, and the Belgians could not make up their minds how to fill it. It was into this situation that Professor A. J. J. van Bilsen hurled his bombshell in 1955. Its effects were instantaneous and permanent.

Van Bilsen, a forty-six-year-old professor at the University Institute for Overseas Territories in Antwerp, has been interested in Africa all his life. He had taken a law doctorate at the Roman Catholic University of Louvain with a view to entering the colonial service. But the outbreak of war diverted his activities into the Belgian freedom and underground struggle, so that he first set foot in the Congo in 1946. He quickly established wide contacts with both Africans and Belgians, and developed an unconventional attitude towards Belgium's proper role in the

Congo. But before expressing any opinions he visited South Africa and other parts of the continent. On his return to the Congo in 1954 he formulated his views in a document entitled 'A Thirty Year Plan for the Political Emancipation of Belgian Africa'. He criticized Belgium for allowing the Congo to be governed with virtually no parliamentary control, and he attacked the unbalanced growth of industrialization on the basis of the American pattern rooted in social paternalism. He contrasted the failure of the Belgian Administration in not training a single African doctor, veterinarian, or engineer with the success of the missions in producing hundreds of priests and a Bishop. 'The Church thus shows', he commented acidly, 'that in the backward countries it is a more dynamic and progressive force than the State.'

But he went much further. 'The colonial imperialism of the past half century is gone forever.' Nor did he lament its passing. Provided the Belgians set about purposefully creating fully democratic and economically viable independent states in the Congo, and in the neighbouring trusteeship territory of Ruanda-Urundi, over a period of thirty years, he felt Belgium's heritage in Africa could be a proud one.

Van Bilsen's timing was absolutely right. In Belgium the Socialist Party was at long last beginning to find its true voice in colonial affairs. The Roman Catholic Church, led by brilliant thinkers like Father van 't Wing, was becoming increasingly aware of the need to put itself on the side of the growing African national consciousness. Both the Socialists and the Roman Catholic hierarchy in the Congo reacted well to van Bilsen's ideas. The Congolese were enthusiastic; it lent them sanction to talk openly about independence. The first major political manifesto of Congo nationalism appeared in the middle of 1956. A group of *évolués*, writing in *Conscience Africaine* (a Catholic-sponsored publication), for the first time spoke openly of political independence for the Congo. 'The colour of one's skin', they said, 'offers no single privilege.' They warned that the concept of a 'Belgian-Congolese Community' was deeply suspect in African minds. But, they quickly added, there was no hostility towards Belgium provided it undertook sincerely and unequivocally to cooperate in achieving Congo's independence within thirty years.

Abako was the next to take up the challenge. The authorship of the *Conscience Africaine* manifesto was largely Bangala; they had gained an initial advantage over the Bakongo by putting themselves in the vanguard of the demand for freedom. Joseph Kasavubu, speaking at a public meeting in August 1956, criticized the *Conscience Africaine* group as being unwilling to forge the political instrument necessary to implement their ideas. 'Our patience', he exclaimed, 'is exhausted. . . . When the hour comes, a nation will not wait.' To recapture the initiative he rejected the proposal that the Congolese should wait for thirty years. But his private views at that time were different. He was open to reasonable negotiations. The Belgians, however, made the mistake of ignoring this demand.

But while the Congo was marking time Africa was not; everywhere along a continental front Pan-Africanism was making gains, and there was no way of preventing the Congolese from knowing about them. Three widely different events can be singled out as the main contributory factors to the 1959 débâcle: General de Gaulle's launching of the French Community; the Brussels World Fair; and the first All-African People's Conference in Accra.

In August 1958, de Gaulle arrived in Brazzaville, on the opposite bank of the Congo to Leopoldville, and gave the French Congolese a choice between membership of the French community as an autonomous republic, or complete independence. The *évolués* in Leopoldville cheered de Gaulle. Two days after his speech, an influential group of *évolués* addressed a respectful but firm memorandum to the Governor-General of the Congo in which they boldly criticized the Government for its failure to include Africans on the study group. 'We fear', they wrote, 'that without the cooperation of the Congolese the study group will produce a unilateral attitude, inspired by conservatism rooted in a spirit of colonialism, which would seriously upset the Africans.' They firmly stated their demand for eventual complete independence.

The leader of this group was Patrice Lumumba, soon to become the Congo's first Prime Minister. Lumumba first appeared in public as chairman of the 'Liberal Friends Circle' in Stanleyville, where he was prominent in *évolué* affairs. Later he was a moving spirit in the *évolué* circles of Leopoldville. Lumumba's group immediately followed up their *démarche* on the Governor-General by creating a new political movement, the Mouvement National Congolais (MNC). It was to become the forerunner of a mushroom growth of smaller parties and movements between the end of 1958 and the beginning of 1959. MNC's aim was to prepare 'the masses and the *élite* to take control of public affairs'; to speed the process of democratization; to implement the Declaration of Human Rights; and, by peaceful negotiation, to do everything possible to free the Congo from colonialism.

In contradistinction to Abako, MNC sought to combat all forms of regional separatism, and to create unity in the higher interests of the Congo as a whole. The drift of Abako towards regional separatism of the Lower Congo continued. Its old opponents, the Bangala, formed a new group, the Union Progressiste Congolaise (UPCO) which pursued the moderate aim of achieving internal autonomy within a Belgian-Congolese Community (rather similar to the idea of the French Community). Like the MNC, UPCO set itself fiercely against attempts to divide the country on tribal or regional lines.

It was during this time that scores of prominent Congolese leaders were invited by the Belgian Government to attend the World Fair in Brussels. There, for the first time, leaders from all parts of the country found themselves in close and continuous association with each other. Previously many of them had never known each other, and knew little or nothing of each other's ideas. One result of this fortuitous gathering was the gradual development of a new political movement, the Mouvement pour le Progrès National Congolais (MPNC).

Although the MPNC was not formally launched until after the Leopoldville riots in the following year its seeding-time was during the critical last few months of 1958. Its leaders were *évolués* studying at the missions in Belgium (a recent innovation), and leaders of *élite* circles in places like Stanleyville, Coquilhatville, Bukavu, Luluabourg, Elizabethville, and Kilo-Moto, as well as Leopoldville. Neither the Abako nor the MNC leaders were associated with it, but the Bangala leaders, always anxious to extend their alliances, were among its most prominent supporters. When it was finally launched the MPNC fully endorsed the Government declaration of policy issued after the Leopold-ville riots. It did not commit itself firmly either to complete independence or to internal autonomy. It emphasized the import-ance of economic and social development, and of national unity. Disunity, it said, would result in 'the return to the stagnation of our races, and to our ancestral poverty'. A weak national move-ment would end in disintegration and a return to tribal wars. Much of the manifesto was couched in the kind of language that finds a great deal of favour with settlers and colonial regimes, causing the movement to be described as 'moderate'.

Finally, there was the third factor which preceded the Leopold-ville upheaval – the All-African People's Conference in Accra on 5 December 1958. The Belgian authorities put no obstacles in the way of the Abako and the MNC leaders who had been invited to attend the conference. But Kasavubu failed to make the trip be-cause his inoculation certificates were not in order; this accident left the way open for Patrice Lumumba and his MNC colleagues to speak for the Congo. They returned to Leopoldville on 28 December, where they addressed an enthusiastic mass meeting. Inspired by Accra's spirit of African solidarity, Lumumba made a full-blooded nationalist speech; he committed the MNC to full support for Accra's decision in favour of immediate independence for all African countries. (The thirty-year programme towards independence was no longer an aim.)

Six days later riots occurred in Leopoldville. Their immediate cause was a march by 30,000 unemployed workers in the city. The Abako leaders were arrested and their movement proscribed. No action was taken against the MNC or other parties. In the twink-ling of an eye the long-delayed reforms for the Congo were announced by the King of the Belgians.

Chapter 6

THE YEAR OF DECISION

*'Kavumenti, the big talker, beats his chest and
swells his lungs – Boasts of riches, boasts of power
tells tall tales that none believe – Kavumenti, empty
windbag, lying tongue and charlatan! Hearken now
and hear the war cry! Hear the war cry loud and
strong!'* *

1959 opened ominously with the riots in Leopoldville which
took the Belgians by surprise; but their rule remained apparently
firmly established. The year closed in gloom and dissension;
Belgian rule was no longer assured, but the nationalists were still
divided and unsure of themselves. Patrice Lumumba was in
prison in Stanleyville.

No colonial power in history was destroyed more quickly, and
by such a rabble: there was not even a coherent nationalist movement which could command nation-wide support. But there was
rebellion; a rebellion of the mind that rejected paternalism and
all it stood for. The children were children no longer.

The Belgians never really understood that it takes two to maintain a true paternalist relationship. When things go wrong between father and son, the parent must be capable either of tyranny
or of changing his attitude; in either case the relationship
changes. When it came to the test the Belgians had no stomach
for tyranny. They tried but failed to change their attitude; and
they ended up muddled, defensive, resentful, and ineffectual.

The riots in Leopoldville had been fierce, and they had been
fiercely repressed by the Force Publique under their white
officers. The same Force Publique was to turn just a year later
on the same officers and their families, and to maltreat them with
equal impartiality. But the riots had been nothing untoward as
riots go in Africa. The total number killed was forty-nine; only
one half the number shot at Sharpeville in South Africa in the

* A Watutsi song recorded by Father Kagamane and translated by
John L. Brown.

following year. It was the mood of the rioters more than anything else that upset the Belgians. For the first time hatred of whites came into the open; missionary property, mainly schools, was specially chosen for destruction.

The brain behind the riots was Joseph Kasavubu's. Moving between the rural stronghold of the Bakongo along the reaches of the Lower Congo, and their urban concentration in Leopoldville, the Abako leader was emerging as the undisputed leader of his tribe; 'King Kasa' soon became a popular salutation. Lumumba was working in Orientale, his home province, to provide a solid base for his national movement. The glory (and the Belgians' disapproval) came to Kasavubu.

Although the riots assumed a political complexion, their causes were primarily economic. The 'blue chip' colony had fallen into financial troubles from 1956 with the decline in the world price of copper and primary commodities. In 1957 the usual budget surplus dropped to a £5 million deficit; by 1958 the deficit had more than trebled, and the outlook was worse for 1959. Unemployment mounted in the large cities, especially in Leopoldville. Demands for action were met by Government denials that the situation was in any way alarming. It was only after the trouble that the serious extent of the Congo's economic decline was admitted. Meanwhile, the social discontent of the unemployed masses in Leopoldville provided Abako with easy material to stir things up; and that is just what the riots succeeded in doing.

Kasavubu and his chief lieutenants were arrested and flown to Belgium, but they were not imprisoned nor were they put on trial. The Belgians sensibly recognized that political trials would only exacerbate the racial feelings inflamed by the riots; they sought to reason with, and to influence, Kasavubu and his colleagues.

If the Belgians had been tardy and indecisive before the riots, they showed less caution when faced with the aftermath. Within a fortnight the King broadcast his now ironically famous speech. Its implications, though heavily tinged with paternalism, were revolutionary. 'The object of our presence in the Dark Continent was thus defined by Leopold II: to open these backward countries to European civilization, to call their peoples to emancipation, liberty, and progress, after having saved them from slavery, disease, and poverty. In continuance of these noble aims, our firm resolve today is to lead, *without fatal evasions but without imprudent haste*, the Congolese peoples to independence in prosperity and peace.' Unfortunately for the intentions of the King, the evasions were fatal, and the haste was imprudent. Less than a year later he himself was compelled to extol the wisdom and statesmanship of granting immediate independence to the Congo.

Despite their mistakes, the Belgians at last got down to making reforms. The long-delayed recommendations of the study group were brought to light: these called for the setting up of restricted Boards of Advisers to the Governor-General and Provincial Governments, which would ultimately become the Council of Ministers, and the creation of a General Council and a Legislative Council as the first stage towards a House of Representatives and a Senate. But the immediate emphasis was on local and provincial government. For the first time elections were promised on a nation-wide basis to secure representative bodies in the lower tiers of government.

In seven months, from January to August, forty Acts and Ordinances containing discriminatory regulations were abolished or changed. The social colour bar was officially pronounced dead; however it still remained very much alive in the European towns. More important, the Congo was given its charter of freedom; for the first time freedom of assembly, of the Press, and of speech was recognized.

The riots had one other important consequence. They finally punctured the propaganda of *Inforcongo*, and awakened the Belgian people to the reality of their responsibilities in the Congo. Like old Rip van Winkle, the Socialist leader of the Belgian parliament, M. Collard, confessed that the people had been stupefied by the events in the Congo. 'January 1959 was the end of an era. But, nevertheless, the Belgians have not yet grasped the importance of these happenings', he told Parliament. 'They are not deeply stirred as yet. As a matter of fact, up to January 1959, the Congo was chiefly a matter concerning financial groups and the administration. Today the Congo is the affair of the Belgian people.'

JUDGE AND JURY

The Belgian Parliament, for the first time too, dispatched an all-party parliamentary commission to discover what had gone wrong in the Congo. Their report was scathing and perceptive; its 100 pages provides a complete exposure of *Inforcongo*. At last the enemy was laid low.

The commission indicted the Congo Government for incompetence, inefficient administration, and indecisiveness. Among the political causes for the riots its report lists the rise of nationalist movements, religious friction, foreign influence (such as the Accra conference), and inadequate news services. Among the social causes it cites human relations between whites and blacks, urban overcrowding resulting from rural migration, unemployment caused by the recession, insufficient schools for children and young people, labour conditions, and the influence exerted by the trade unions.

But the most valuable part of the commission's report is its chapter on race relations. Here is a warning for the multi-racial societies in Africa that continue to delude themselves still, as the Belgians had done for so long, that the Africans really wish for nothing more than to be guided by the whites; that they desire only the continuation of white leadership, and respect its policies; that the daily grievances and feelings of humiliation can be safely contained within a system of repressive law and disciplined order.

The commission defined three stages in the evolution of a colony under white rule. The first phase follows on the period of occupation and pacification: the presence of the white man is accepted without discussion; he gives the orders and is obeyed; the rulers accept that they know the wishes of the natives. In the second phase, the white man's sense of responsibility for the black man grows weaker. 'Blacks are increasingly looked upon as workers with no personality of their own; they must be educated and instructed, though chiefly to increase the value of their labour; they are turned into skilled workers and clerks. At this time the whites in the larger centres have no other relations with the blacks than is necessary for their employment. The blacks make no complaints; they submit themselves without opposition to the privileges enjoyed by the whites. But, gradually, as they become more efficient in their work, their intellectual vision rises and they begin to see things in a different light.' The third phase comes with the declaration of human rights and the emancipation of colonies. Things grow more difficult. 'The whites are bound to a society in which the colour of one's skin plays an important role; on the other hand, the black *évolués* seek the immediate eradication of all colour bars.'

The commission moves on from this incisive analysis to consider the effects of deteriorating human relations. The whites become divided in their attitudes to the new situation; some become aware of the need for a new relationship; many remain indifferent; others poison relations by their words and actions. The *petit blancs*, the less-privileged among the whites, feel threatened by the rise of the *évolués* claiming their lower-paid jobs; they assume an attitude of superiority unsoftened by psychological insights. Moreover, it is this group which is in closest contact with the blacks in their daily lives.

On the other hand, the *évolués* – who become the political leaders – are not always ready to bring about any improvement in human relations either. They screw up their grievances. The absence of genuine social mixing leads them to doubt the sincerity of the authorities' intentions. 'The individual feelings of vengeance and of grievance are progressively increased; daily the dissatisfaction rises and is exploited by black leaders in whose interests it is to spread hate against the Europeans. At the first opportunity the hatred explodes.'

That was the lesson of the Leopoldville riots. But an even more important lesson learned by the commission was summed up in a single sentence: '*In a country where the white man is both judge and jury, it is human that the black man should begin to feel that he can get no justice because he is black.*'

PLOTS AND INTRIGUES

The Belgians' prompt reaction to the riots, and their acutely honest attempts to draw the right lessons, successfully restored the initiative that had slipped from their fingers. But they now had to contend with new forces called into play by the events of the first few months of 1959. African politicians were now in an assertive mood, competing with each other for influence and leadership. The *colons* were alarmed by the prospect of a 'sell-out'. In Brussels a right-wing lobby began to react through intrigues in the Palace and in the Chamber of Representatives.

The man entrusted to push through the New Deal was M. Maurice van Hemelrijck, who had become Minister of the Belgian Congo a few months before the Leopoldville riots. He is an exceptional politician, tough, skilled, and independent-minded. His reputation stood high because of his successful handling of the religious conflict over education in Belgium. He had few illusions about what needed to be done. In the Congo he talked to Africans, to administrators, to businessmen, and to the *colons*. 'I keep repeating the word *independence* on purpose, even though it may have unpleasant associations for some people. We must not be afraid of words; we must be far more wary of complexes, rancour, trouble, hypocrisy, and bluster.' The Africans cheered him; the *colons* attacked him, and he had to be protected from them by the Force Publique. The administration was wary; and the businessmen were divided.

It soon became obvious that it was easier to define the Congo's new policy than to implement it. The Governor-General had to be replaced, and right-wing pressures mollified. Congolese leaders again became suspicious; they were particularly wary of the idea of the Belgian-Congolese Community which M. van Hemelrijck kept stressing. Astute politician that he is, the Minister had realized by the middle of 1959 that, far from slowing down the pace of reform, the need was to speed it up. Only in this way could the moderate Congolese leaders be assured of electoral victory. He had also concluded that law and order in a deteriorating situation could be successfully reimposed only with the support of Congolese leaders. Once convinced of the importance of granting a wide measure of responsibility in the central legislature, the Minister moved swiftly towards its realization. But he failed to carry his colleagues with him.

The right-wing lobby in Brussels, with its anxious interest in 'not going too fast', intensified its pressures and intrigues, and

M. van Hemelrijck was compelled to resign in September. He was succeeded by M. A. E. de Schrijver, a politician experienced in Congolese affairs, and one, so it was thought, who would move with less impetuosity than his predecessor. As so often happens, in the end he moved even faster; the disasters foreseen by M. van Hemelrijck if attempts were made to slow down reforms became reality. For while the *colons* and the right-wing business interests rejoiced in his downfall, the Congolese interpreted it as a Belgian 'evasion'; for them it was a sign that Belgium was getting ready to retreat from its promises. They intensified their demands and moved their targets forwards towards immediate and complete independence.

M. van Hemelrijck was to say later to the Catholic Flemish Club at Lier: 'The drama was that those who thought I was busy losing the Congo were themselves contributing most towards the result.' He denounced the freemasons and certain financial interests who had set themselves up to work actively against him, and he went on to make these interesting disclosures: 'I proposed immediate elections to establish a constitution with an African Government, with the proviso that the Congo need not become a unitary state but could become a federation. I came up against the opposition of former Ministers of the Colonies. Behind my back somebody was sent to the Congo to take the pulse of the people there. My dismissal provoked concern among the blacks. My successor, the best and experienced of statesmen, was also of the opinion that my policy went too far. Since then, however, the most advanced opinion in the Congo has imposed its will. The extremists have come into power in place of the former leaders.'

The Belgians never recovered from the mistake of M. van Hemelrijck's dismissal. The tardy, the fearful, and the conservative-minded had a brief, inglorious victory. The temporary initiative was finally lost in September 1959, and the 'drama of the Congo' moved swiftly to its fateful climax.

Chapter 7

THE BIRTH OF POLITICS

'If we could have counted at this moment on proper organizations at a provincial level, the political solutions for the Congo would have been greatly facilitated. Indeed, it is a political mistake that has been made in the past.'

M. EYSKENS, Prime Minister of Belgium
(January, 1960)

RIGHT from the beginning Congo politics foreshadowed the polarization between what might be called 'tribal nationalism' and 'Pan-African nationalism'; the former insists on a single tribe as the centre of growth, while the latter seeks to achieve a national unity transcending tribal loyalties.

Abako, the first party formed in 1956, is rooted as is implied by its full name – the Association of the Bakongo for the Unification, Conservation and Expansion of Likongo (their language) – in the 800,000 Bakongo tribesmen living in the Lower Congo. At the opposite pole is the Mouvement National Congolais (MNC), founded by Patrice Lumumba in 1958. It eschewed tribalism from the start, concentrating on a unifying Congolese nationalism. Tribal nationalism found its natural expression in federalism, Pan-African nationalism in unitarianism. This struggle is the crux of Congo politics; it divides those who wish for a strong unitary state from those wanting a federal system of largely autonomous provincial governments based on primary tribal alliances.

This conflict is a phenomenon of modern Africa. It is crystallized in what happened in Ghana and Nigeria. In Ghana, Dr Kwame Nkrumah triumphed in his demand for centralized government; to achieve it he had to overcome the federalist demands of the Ashanti, the tribal chiefs in the Northern Territories, and the Ewe nationalists in Togoland. In Nigeria, the nationalist demands of Dr Nnamde Azikiwe were defeated by the insistence of Chief Awolowo and of the Muslim Emirs that

Nigeria should become a federation of its three major regions. It was a feature, too, of the Sudan in the first year of its independence. A similar struggle is being waged between the nationalists of Uganda and their traditional rulers.

Centralism versus federalism has bedevilled politics in the Old World for centuries. It may do the same in Africa. So far, experience shows that it is easier for the unitarians to win in small countries like Ghana than in larger countries like Nigeria. The Congo has much more in common with the latter than the former. Theoretically, therefore, the advantage in politics should have been with the federalists in the Congo; but it was the unitarians, in fact, who made most of the running. They were still ahead when independence came. Only then were they checked; whether temporarily or otherwise still remains to be seen.

PEOPLES AND REGIONS

It will be easier to follow the growth of political movements and ideas if some explanation is made of the natural ethnic and physical conditions of the Congo. The country covers an area of 900,000 square miles with a population at independence of 13,500,000 Africans and 113,000 whites, of whom 89 per cent were Belgians. The Congolese are divided into seventy major ethnic groups, each of which is subdivided into hundreds of tribes and clans. More than 400 dialects are in active use. Apart from French, known mainly to the urban-dwellers, there is no *lingua franca*, although Kiswahili is widely spoken in the eastern parts, and Lingala in the west.

Nearly one-quarter of the Congolese are now urbanized; the two largest centres are Leopoldville with 350,000, and Elizabethville with 200,000 inhabitants. The effects, if not necessarily the intention, of Belgian policy has been to develop separate tribal governments based on district councils. The practice, if not the theory, of this policy bears a striking resemblance to Dr Verwoerd's ideas of Bantustans in South Africa. Tribal loyalties have been fostered in the Congo, and have remained strong even when the rural dwellers migrate to the towns.

The country is divided into six administrative provinces. There are many different tribes in each province; usually they dwell together in sections comprising their traditional lands. Each province is distinguished by the presence within it of one or two dominant tribes. Each of the provinces has developed its own characteristics which are only partly explained historically.

Katanga is the area of mining and industrial development, lying on the south-eastern frontier with Northern Rhodesia. Elizabethville is only a short distance from the towns of the Rhodesian Copperbelt, and there is a measure of political affinity between the whites of Katanga and those of Rhodesia. The Congolese population is 1,650,000, with a white population at independence of 33,500. As an industrial magnet it attracted workers from all parts of the Congo. One effect of this immigration was that the indigenous people of Katanga, the Luvale, felt themselves numerically threatened by outsiders. There is also a strong concentration of Baluba, partly incomers from Kasai, and partly established in a region of their own. This tribe is also strong in neighbouring Kasai.

Equator – a remote and comparatively undeveloped area lying well outside the mainstream of economic and political development, with Coquilhatville as capital – has a population of 1,800,000 Congolese, and fewer than 7,000 whites at independence.

Orientale revolves mainly around its expanding and lively capital, Stanleyville (Patrice Lumumba's home ground). It has a Congolese population of 2,500,000 and, up to independence, an expanding white population of 16,500.

Kivu, the scenically splendid and temperate region, is in a minor sense the 'White Highlands' of the Congo. Officially encouragement was given at one time to white settlement there. But its white population stood at only 14,000 at independence, while its Congolese population, organized into a number of powerful Chiefdoms, totalled 2,260,000.

Kasai, plumb in the middle of the Congo, is the home of the Lulua, a proud and self-conscious tribe who cling tenaciously to their traditional life of hunting and farming; they cared little in the past for education or Christianity, and even less for working for whites. Their conservatism gave an opening to the ambitious Baluba tribe to play an increasingly important role in the expanding economy of the province; a fact deeply resented by the Lulua on the eve of independence. The Congolese population totals 2,345,000; the white population was 9,000 at independence.

Leopoldville province includes the region of the Lower Congo, the home of the Bakongo, the most sophisticated of Congolese tribes. It also includes the Kwango-Kwilo peoples, who are even more numerous than the Bakongo. The rapid growth of the city of Leopoldville attracted large numbers of immigrants from the Upper Congo. The Congolese population is 3,200,000, and there were 33,600 whites at independence.

MUSHROOM GROWTH OF PARTIES

The growth of political parties when they came strongly reflected these provincial and tribal divisions. After the long drought of colonial paternalism, the 1959 Charter granting freedom of speech, press, and association produced a splurge of parties. They sprang up everywhere; nobody was going to be left out of the new opportunity to stake a claim in the promised political Kingdom; everybody was ready to serve some special interest of his own.

There were those who supported Lumumba's idea of a national movement; they formed branches of their own, not necessarily recognizing the authority of MNC. There were tribal parties, and federations of parties of the smaller tribes. There were provincial regional parties. There were federations of inter-provincial parties. There were parties to 'defend the rights of the peasants and other rural dwellers'. There was a Labour Party and a Liberal Party. There were parties to defend 'the ancient customs and traditions of the Chiefs and their peoples'. There were inter-racial parties, such as the Rassemblement Congolais in Katanga, which sought 'to maintain the higher ideals of European civilization'. And there were parties initiated and fostered by settlers and by the Administration – an example of the former was Moise Tshombe's Conakat Party, and of the latter, the Parti National du Progrès (PNP).

This vivid array of parties changed pattern with bewildering speed. They renamed themselves, altered their objects, and made and broke alliances. They threw up new leaders continuously.

Many lost their identities completely by forming wider associations. Finally they boiled themselves down from literally hundreds of parties to a reasonable thirty or so. Broadly speaking they supported four tendencies: separatist regionalism (as exemplified by Kasavubu's Abako in the Lower Congo); federalism (support for six autonomous states within a central framework, as Tshombe's Conakat); immediate and unconditional independence (demanded by Lumumba's MNC); independence within the framework outlined by the Belgian Government.

None of the parties was against Europeans as such, but they were practically all against European domination. A 1959 survey by Dr George Brausch* found that 'the new political parties were a reaction against the paternalism of European political parties ... and thus the basic tendency of these nationalist movements is opposition to European domination. Nevertheless, most of the nationalist movements have European counsellors, even the extremist [sic] MNC, Abako, and the People's Party – and all admit Europeans to membership.'

This survey emphasized a vital point which, even in 1959, the Administration refused to come to terms with: the universality with which the idea of European domination had been rejected. Constitutional reforms that did not hold out the prospect of representative government could not possibly succeed. This spirit had been recognized by M. van Hemelrijck, and it still found a faint echo in the policy outlined in October 1959 by the new Congo Minister, M. de Schrijver. 'Belgium desires that in 1960 the Congo shall have its own government, borough and urban councils.'

But Belgium's desires were being scantly regarded by the Congolese, who had begun to assert their own desires. Many – though by no means all – were strongly dissatisfied with the timetable produced by Belgium: communal and territorial elections in December 1959; indirect elections for the Provincial Councils in March 1960; indirect elections for a Central Government in September 1960. Nobody spoke then about the immutable right of 'one man, one vote'. But many objected violently to the continuation of indirect elections, leaving the right of the

* Director of the Solvay Katanga Centre of Social Research at Elizabethville.

people's choice to the primary elections of local government. The 'independence-now' parties were making the running, with the moderate parties trying to put on the brake, strongly assisted by the Administration. But a different kind of threat, not mentioned publicly at the time by any official quarter, was building up in the Lower Congo.

KASA'S KINGDOM

Kasavubu's plans to create a single tribal authority owing its allegiance to Abako had made considerable progress. His personal authority, though not yet decisive, was enormous. We now know from official sources how critical the position was that faced the Administration in the Lower Congo in 1959; the extent of the deterioration was hidden at the time. Abako's passive resistance campaign, dismissed as 'intimidation', had, in fact become a popular movement. Refusal to pay taxes was widespread. Accused and plaintiffs refused to answer summonses to appear in the native traditional courts; tribal judges, too, stayed away. The Abako operated its own system of courts. All administrative measures dealing with land and health were ignored.

The Administration had clearly begun to lose its grip on the situation; worse than that, Abako was succeeding in setting up its independent, parallel administration. In the competition for allegiance between the two, Abako was winning. It was not only the administrators who were worried; businessmen in the Lower Congo were beginning to feel the pressure. Some joined the Abako as members; many more subscribed to it. Among the missions – both Catholic and Protestant – there was strong support for Abako, and competition for influence. The Jesuits, in particular, supported Kasavubu. The Protestants supported his chief lieutenant, Daniel Kanza. But there was a third religious influence, nascent rather than active – Kibanguism.

Simon Kibangu was a Protestant teacher, who had set himself up in 1921 as the Messiah. With his twelve Apostles he taught a tribal religion opposed both to Christianity and to the Europeans. His movement spread rapidly among the Bakongo, and it was put down only after many years of turbulence. Although there had been many Christian breakaway sects in the Congo, none had flourished so strongly as Kibangu's. It was finally crushed with great severity. Kibangu, given a life sentence, died a repentant Roman Catholic in 1956. But his belated conversion and death did not spell the end of Kibanguism. Its religious teachings had political undertones that became dominant in Abako's teaching. Although its leaders did not share the anti-white racialism of many of Abako's supporters (Kasavubu and Kanza both remain staunchly attached to their Christian faith), they nevertheless had to take account of the influence of Kibanguism. Kasavubu managed, without the reproach of the Church, to establish a close relationship with the Kibanguists.

Abako's appeal was twofold. It called forth the tribal nationalism of the Bakongo, and it asserted a spirit of independence against Belgian domination. Kasavubu's dream of restoring the ancient Bakongo Kingdom by eliminating the colonial frontiers which divided the tribe into three, provided a romantic impulse to the independence movement. After the Leopoldville riots and Kasavubu's triumphant return from his brief exile in Belgium, he found himself hailed as the King of the Bakongo. Stripping himself of his *évolué* clothes, he would appear before his enthusiastic followers dressed in traditional leopard skin.

By the end of 1959 the position of the Belgians in the Lower Congo had grown almost hopeless. Their authority could be restored only by military force. But could it be successfully restored? The prospect of a colonial war could not be lightly viewed. In normal circumstances it might have been possible for the Belgians to undertake a repressive campaign to deal with the dissidents. But the situation was not normal. There could be no assurance that a large-scale war in the Lower Congo would not be the signal for risings in other parts of the Congo. All the signs supported the view that a general revolt might easily occur. It was one of the strongest factors in the minds of the Belgians in determining their subsequent policies.

MONTHS OF TWILIGHT

1959 ended as it had begun – in bloodshed. The first serious inter-tribal fighting had broken out in Kasai in the middle of the year between the Lulua and the Baluba. With the unfamiliar prospect of self-government, albeit provincial, opening up before them, the Lulua tribesmen suddenly discovered that, through all the years while they had followed the hunt and lazed in the indolence of tribal pastoralism, the Baluba had zestfully entered the new society; they had become strongly entrenched in the white man's world. If the white man went, the Baluba would be in a strong position to take over and impose their authority on the Lulua who, traditionally, had dominated that part of the world until the Belgians came. The Lulua tribal leaders decided the time had come to assert their right to power; their followers interpreted this as a sign to drive the Baluba intruders out of their capital, Luluabourg. The Belgians were awkwardly caught between the spears and the arrows of the conflicting sides. M. van Hemelrijck (who was still Minister of the Congo at the time) was horrified by the responsibility Belgian officials had to carry for dealing with this violence. It was another reason he subsequently gave for his decision to transfer a large measure of responsibility on to the Congolese themselves.

The October statement* by his successor, M. de Schrijver, set off a strenuous competition between the political parties: the 'extremists' rejected his timetable for constitutional advancement, and called for the proposed elections in December to be postponed pending further consultations; the 'moderates' welcomed the proposal. In this rivalry Lumumba showed himself to be the leader of the extreme elements; he was, indeed, most impatient of any delay in granting independence. His demands had grown to outright and immediate independence, thus splitting his party. Albert Kalonji, the Baluba leader in the Diamond District of Kasai, denounced his leader's 'immoderation', formed his own right wing within the MNC, and joined the ranks of the federalists. The contest between the moderates and extremists produced an explosion in Stanleyville where M. Lumumba was campaigning. He was arrested and sentenced to six months' imprisonment. Later he complained of severe police ill-treatment; to prove it he was able to show the unhealed scars on his wrists when he was brought to Brussels in January 1960 to attend the Round Table conference.

The decision to hold this conference in Brussels with the

* See page 68.

Congolese leaders was taken by the Belgian Government in a last desperate effort to retrieve once again the initiative they had lost during the year. The Congo was drifting towards anarchy; Belgian power was no longer able to maintain the law and order which for so long they had managed to keep with such exemplary if stern efficiency. It was time to decide the country's future.

Chapter 8

FIGHT OR ABDICATE

*'Does anybody really think, in view of the realities
of the situation and the nature of the problem, that
the Government, any Government, could have acted
differently? It is inevitable that the Congo should
evolve to independence and it is impossible to prevent it from acquiring this new kind of political
freedom. The Government has done right to show a
generous attitude in conceding independence.'*

M. EYSKENS, Belgian Prime Minister
(February, 1960)

THE Round Table Conference opened in Brussels on 20 January
1960. Within a week the fate of the Congo was sealed: it was to
become completely independent within six months. The Belgians
were completely unprepared for the swiftness with which events
had moved.

But it was not only the Belgians who were unprepared. The
news reached the second All-African People's Conference in
Tunis soon after its opening. Everybody in the hall was silent for
a moment; then the applause broke loose. It was a memorable
moment in the history of Pan-Africanism. Only a short year
earlier Patrice Lumumba had appeared on its platform at the
first conference in Accra; then he was an unknown leader from a
country without a nationalist movement. Who could have predicted the swift transformation of his, and of the Congo's fortunes? Certainly not the Belgian Prime Minister. In opening the
Round Table Conference his speech, though accommodating,
was self-assured. 'You, the delegates of the Congo, are present in
order to talk with us. From the bottom of our hearts we beg you
to speak without fear: let yourselves be guided only by what you
esteem is for the good of all the Congolese people. Speak to us
freely and without bitterness . . . at the start we are all agreed on
one essential factor – the Congo's independence.'

On that point there *was* agreement; but on what terms? The

Belgians did not envisage immediate independence. They believed it was possible to achieve a Belgian-Congolese Community. They hoped, too, that their King might still be recognized as King of an independent Congo. What had gone wrong? As usually happens when a nation suffers from self-deception, the Belgians could not even then bring themselves to understand the extent of Congolese opposition to their continued rule. And, as invariably happens too, in similar situations, their political intelligence reflected what the Government wanted to believe. The reports were that the 'extremists' demanding immediate independence were in a tiny minority. All that was needed was to arrange a 'representative' conference, where the results could be made to speak for themselves. They did; but not in the way the Belgians had intended.

The conference was attended by 81 Congolese delegates – 62 to represent about 20 parties, and 19 delegates to represent tribal and traditional elements. Of the 62 politicians 32 could reasonably be relied upon to take a 'moderate' line; this was more or less guaranteed by the Congo Administration. The bulk of these comprised 22 delegates in the coalition of the Parti National du Progrès (PNP) which was directly financed and guided by the Administration. Their support, together with the tribal and traditional elements should, in normal circumstances, have ensured a 'properly weighted' conference. It was neatly calculated. Only one factor had been overlooked: the pressure of Congolese nationalism. Not even the 'moderates' dared to face their supporters without having pledged themselves to immediate independence. The success of the 'independence now' movement in the December elections* had finally brought that truth home to the Congolese, if not yet to the Belgians.

* The election in December 1959 had taken place despite the opposition to it. In Leopoldville the boycott of Abako and its then ally, PSA, was almost complete. In Orientale, Lumumba's candidates won the urban areas, while the PNP held its ground in the rural areas. In Kasai, Kalonji's MNC and the Lulua tribal organization shared the victory. In Katanga, Tshombe's Conakat won a majority, but Balubakat polled well. In Kivu the PNP tendency appeared to have won against the nationalist-minded CEREA. And in Equator the PNP forces won against a determined bid by the MNC. On the face of it these results showed strong, but by no means decisive, support for the Administration-sponsored PNP; but they foreshadowed the rising fortunes of Lumumba, the strength of Tshombe in Katanga, and the power of Abako in the Lower Congo.

The Belgians' unpreparedness is shown by their proposal that the question of independence be deferred until later in the agenda. The challenge that it should be taken first was easily carried. The unexpected happened. There was a *unanimous* demand for complete independence. Faced with this demand the Belgians had to decide: either they must accept or fight.

The Belgian Government (a coalition between the Christian Social Party and the Liberals) was temperamentally inclined against repression; Catholic interests favoured concessions, as did an influential section of Big Business. King Baudouin, too, was under strong liberal influences. And the Government was under no illusions about the dangers already threatening them in the Lower Congo. They accepted the demand for complete independence.

But the second blow struck them even more sharply: a motion that independence should be achieved on 30 June 1960 was carried by an overwhelming majority. By then it was too late to resist, even if the will to do so had been there. The Belgians decided to rely on gratitude for their past achievements, on the indisputable need for continued Belgian financial and technical aid, and on the goodwill that would be earned by a spirit of generosity in conceding immediate independence. These factors, they believed would ensure close cooperation between an independent Congo and themselves. If things subsequently went wrong, the reasons must be looked for in deeper causes. On the face of it, the Belgian decision was boldly realistic. In fact, they had no alternative (as the Prime Minister later said) once they found the Congolese leaders completely agreed on the vital principles. A closer examination of what happened at the Round Table Conference provides some clues for the Belgians' subsequent failure.

BLACK FACES IN BRUSSELS

The atmosphere in Brussels in January 1960 was decidedly unusual. The sight of black faces in the city was comparatively rare, because it had been the policy of the Belgians not to allow Congolese to study, or rarely even to visit, Europe. The sight of two hundred* black faces in the streets and squares and hotels of

* Although there were only eighty-one official delegates, most parties sent teams of advisers as well.

Brussels made the *presence* of the Congo a reality for the majority
of the Belgians for the first time in their lives. People stood un-
ashamedly and stared; with the help of pictures in their daily
papers – suddenly given over to front-page coverage of the doings
and sayings of the hitherto anonymous Congolese – they tried to
spot the different personalities. When I was walking one day with
Patrice Lumumba a woman came up and asked him who he was.
'There,' she said triumphantly, 'I told you it was that man
Lumumba.'

The Belgians seemed to enjoy their personal discovery of the
Congolese as much as their guests enjoyed Brussels despite its
intense, bright coldness. The younger delegates took over a
down-town café and turned it into a nightly haunt for African
dancing and singing. It became the social venue for Congolese
of all parties. Many of the leaders were now meeting each other
for the first time, and making friends – or enemies. One Sunday
morning I sat patiently by for half an hour in the foyer of a
Brussels hotel while Moise Tshombe, foolishly elegant and suave,
loudly lectured Lumumba; that argument ended with Lumumba
saying three crisp sentences to Tshombe, who treated his curt
dismissal with pleasant good humour.

Lumumba had been flown straight from prison to Brussels after
the decision on independence had been taken. The Belgians were
clearly embarrassed by the evidence of ill-treatment he showed on
his arrival; the official explanation was that his handcuffs had
been rather roughly twisted when he had refused to obey a command. But Lumumba's mood was all forgiveness and friendship;
there was no evidence of any feeling that one good twist deserved
another. Lumumba quickly became the popular figure at the
conference. He was lodged in room 53 in the Cosmopolitan
Hotel. It was a small, plain room with two plain narrow beds,
both too short for the length of their occupant. There were two
narrow tables, covered with bottles of vitamin tablets, and
strewn with scraps of paper on which were scribbled designs for
an independence flag. The half-open cupboard door showed two
extra suits and two pairs of shoes. The telephone never stopped
ringing; young men padded in and out of the room constantly;
some of them went barefooted and wore their early morning
pyjamas.

I found Lumumba's attitude at that time distinctly cooperative, though inflexible on some points. Despite constant interruptions he talked without losing his thread for several hours. 'In a young state you must have strong and visible powers. Mistakes have been made in the past, but we now want to set up, with the help of the powers who have been in Africa, a powerful *bloc*. If this does not happen, it will be the fault of the West. We are friendly to the West which has helped us up to now. In the future our relations must be based on equality. We can walk hand in hand with the West to construct in Black Africa a grand, well-organized society.' He spoke of his great attachment to Dr Nkrumah. 'I have been greatly impressed by Nkrumah's praise for the British.'

The second Congo Headquarters was at the ritzy Plaza Hotel where the Abako delegation stayed. Unlike Lumumba's, Kasavubu's room was large and elegantly decorated in Regency red-and-white striped wallpaper, with satin curtains and coverings. But he was much more difficult to talk to at first. He sat squatly in a stiff chair, his chunky body tense, his short, thick legs planted firmly on the ground. He peered stolidly from behind thick lenses. Two good-looking, courteous young acolytes sat uneasily on one of the beds, interrupting only when appealed to for confirmation of what their leader was saying. Below us a Sunday afternoon tea-dance was going on. The lobby of the hotel was full of delegates and of strangers firmly stuck behind their papers: some were plain-clothes policemen keeping an eye on what was going on; others were 'contact men' trying to nobble the delegates with promises of foreign aid and propositions for commercial transactions.

Kasavubu had just come in from an Abako caucus meeting that had started at ten that morning and finished at four o'clock. It was typical of the strain under which everybody was working. Unlike Lumumba he had not a good word to say for the Belgians. 'They have agreed to talk at last, but they are not willing to give us the means to achieve independence. The Belgian authorities have committed suicide. There is a complete lack of confidence in the Administration. They are no longer capable of carrying on, but they are also not prepared to let anybody else carry on. There must obviously be some time for preparation, but this requires some transitional power other than the Belgians'. There are no national parties in the Congo, other than those organized by the Administration, such as the PNP. Originally the Administration also encouraged the MNC, but that is no longer the case. The question of a single, united Congo is simply a matter of "words". Whatever the "word", there will be unity. There is no question of Abako not cooperating to achieve the country's unity. I never wanted to separate the Lower Congo from the rest of the country to form a separate Kingdom. That is simply colonialist propaganda against me. They even go so far as to call me a communist.'

I asked him why the Belgians had changed their policies in the Congo. He explained that 'in the past the Belgians did not have enough contact with the people to know what was really happening, and did not heed even the information they received. They were surprised to discover how strong the spirit of independence had become. Every Congo leader has been caught up in this spirit. Now it is 30 June, whether independence works or not. There is no question of delaying it.'

Why was he suspicious of the Belgians? 'They are still trying to divide everybody. Only a provisional government can organize proper elections. No elections organized by the Belgian Administration can succeed.' Was he in the pay of foreigners as was being alleged? 'This is simply propaganda against me. Admittedly my family live in Brazzaville, the capital of the French Congo, but they have lived there a long time.'

His policy was 'an open door for all countries to help in the Congo. For the moment we are all nationalists. We will guarantee the Belgians' economic interests.' His advocacy, of a loose federation was to promote true national unity. 'As national unity developed it would be possible to strengthen the central institutions. Congolese feelings of oneness are only now beginning.'

AFRICANS BAD AND GOOD

The Belgian Press had cast Kasavubu in the role of the Bad African: day after day he was accused of plotting with Belgium's enemies. Although he was seen daily with Professor van

Bilsen,* he was charged with working with the agents of M. Sou-
stelle, France's arch-reactionary, with a view to 'stealing' the
Lower Congo (the site of the Inga project) for the French Congo.
In those days Kasavubu was certainly seeing lots of people, and
some of them were 'strange'. He had made a mysterious trip to
France, but returned without staying there. Kasavubu was quite
willing, however, to clear up the mystery. 'I want to make sure,'
he told me at the time, 'that when the Congo becomes independent we will not have to rely only on the Belgians.'

Kasavubu had started the conference in a strong position. He
secured the initiative by forming a Cartel (a coalition of parties)
between Abako, the Kalonji wing of MNC, and the Parti Solidaire Africain (the second largest party in Leopoldville province).
This gave him the support of twenty-two of the sixty-two political
delegates. His strength equalled that of the officially approved
PNP. Lumumba's MNC at first had only three delegates. Tshombe
was running his own ticket with four delegates. The other eleven
delegates belonged to four different parties.

In the first week of the conference Kasavubu lost his initiative
through tactical mistakes. Not only did he succeed in splitting
the Abako Cartel, he split his own party as well. The Protestant
wing of the Abako, led by Daniel Kanza and his sons, joined in
the Belgian attack on him as 'the agent of foreign powers'.
Kasavubu withdrew from the conference, threatening to boycott
it unless it agreed to create an interim government immediately
to whom authority could be entrusted to run the country and to
prepare for elections. He also demanded an immediate decision
on the federal future of the independent Congo. His tactics
united the conference against him. In the end he was compelled
to return to the conference table, but by then he had lost his
formidable position. Lumumba took the initiative from Kasavubu, and his only effective rivals were the PNP.

The PNP was the force on which the Belgians were staking
their future, covering themselves with a side-bet on Lumumba's

* Professor A. J. J. van Bilsen, who enjoys the confidence of the Catholic
hierarchy, was the author of the Thirty Year Plan for Congo independence
(see page 52) which, at the time of its publication in 1955, was condemned
by the authorities as being dangerously idealistic and wildly unrealistic.
How distant his 'radical' plans for independence by 1985 seemed in January 1960!

MNC. The rank outsider was Abako. The split in its ranks was gleefully hailed; well-informed circles confidently predicted that the Kanza faction would win and that Kasavubu would disappear from the scene. Once again their predictions were to be proved wrong. PNP was to be defeated, and Kasavubu was to defeat his opponents in Abako with hardly a struggle. The Belgian Press made no secret of the Administration's support for the PNP; their leaders were praised and courted. But the Conakat leader, Moise Tshombe, was by no means popular. Officials and the Press said quite openly that he was being subsidized by certain financial interests, whose tactics they deplored. It was only much later that Tshombe, for a fleeting moment, became the darling of Brussels.

The Belgian line was now plain. It was to encourage support for the 'moderates', especially the PNP and the traditional elements who might be relied upon to follow a pro-Belgian policy; to work quietly for a Belgian-Congolese Community after independence; to promote the idea of a common loyalty to the Crown; to safeguard the integrity of the country after independence, and to ensure the safety of Belgian economic interests. These objectives were to be achieved in several ways: by treaties guaranteeing Belgium's legitimate interests; by underpinning the Administration and economic development through the provision of technical and financial aid, and by attracting foreign capital. The Belgians also insisted on the retention of their military bases. They really saw themselves administering the country under an African Government, until such time as the Congolese were ready to take over themselves. This was precisely what the dismissed Minister of the Congo, M. van Hemelrijck, had envisaged nine months earlier. The difference was that the initiative still lay partly with the Belgians when he had proposed it; by the time his ideas came to be accepted the initiative had been lost. But for many Belgians the only question of real importance that remained was how best to protect their vast economic interests in the Congo.

HOSTAGE TO FORTUNE

Estimates of Belgian investments and commitments in the Congo vary greatly; nor is it easy to disentangle the precise inter-relationship of the economies of the two countries. Belgium's financial involvement in the Congo has been variously put at between £1,500 millions and £2,450 millions, depending on what is taken into calculation, and what valuation is put on shareholdings. At the beginning of 1959 the value of shares owned by Belgian investors in colonial enterprises was officially given as £420 millions. This figure did not include investments in private enterprises – factories, restaurants, hotels, buildings, farming, and commercial trading concerns.

The growth of political uncertainty in 1959 had set off a wild flight of capital from the Congo; by the end of that year it exceeded £35 million. In 1960 it was running at the rate of £7 million a month before the Belgians finally decided to intervene. They persuaded the principal financial groups to transfer some of their capital back to the Congo, and to make *advance* payments to the colony's Treasury representing future taxes, duties, and dividends amounting to £17,500,000. This policy in effect pledged the country's future earnings to meeting its past and current deficits, thus seriously threatening the future liquidity of the independent Congo's finances, already heavily burdened by service charges on its public debt.

At the beginning of 1960 the Congo Government was faced with a £40 million deficit, the result of three years of declining fortunes caused by the drop in world commodity prices since 1956. To this figure must be added a further £30 million which was the estimated deficit for 1960 – an estimate made before the catastrophe. To help meet these enormous deficits the Belgians had roused themselves to an unprecedented national effort. They proposed to grant the Congo a subsidy in 1960 amounting to nearly £19 million, apart from £4 million allocated to the Investment Fund of the Overseas Territories of the European Economic Community, and £7 million pledged to the creation of a Belgo-Congolese Development Corporation. But these subsidies, amounted to less than half the deficits of 1956–9.

Nor did this constitute the full liabilities to be assumed by the first Congo Government. It inherited a Public Debt of £350 million which had been raised and guaranteed by the Belgians. The servicing and redemption of this Debt required almost 25 per cent of the Congo's annual budget, far and away the highest debt burden bequeathed to any of the former African colonies. There are two softening features about the size of this Debt. First, the Congo Government inherited a Portfolio of assets valued at about £240 million, comprising a large slice of the holdings in the Union Minière, and outright ownership of several large public utilities; but this inheritance contributed nothing to ensuring the immediate liquidity of the new Government. Secondly, full allowance should be made for the fact that the greatest part of the Debt had been incurred in development work within the Congo.*

Belgian economic policy in the Congo was laid down in 1908 when parliament, in agreeing to take the country over from the King, decided that the finances of the two countries should be kept entirely separate. The justification for this policy was that Belgium should not profit from the Congo. But this attractive-sounding proposition ignored the vast benefits the Belgian economy derived from the colony's resources. Apart from profits on investment (which, it might properly be argued, represented normal business returns), Belgium thrived on the fabulous gold earnings derived from Congo exports. For example, the Congo contributed greatly towards sustaining the Belgian economy throughout the Second World War. It was not altogether a one-sided deal; the Congo benefited, for example, by its ability to raise capital on the strength of Belgium's security. But the balance of advantage decidedly favoured the Belgians as *Inforcongo* admitted in 1959. Nevertheless she made no monetary contributions to the Congo until 1959.

Belgium's financial relations with her colony were criticized from the outset. Thus, early in 1909, E. D. Morel raised important questions in a memorandum sent to the British Government on behalf of the Congo Reform Association.† He pointed out that the colony was already then saddled with an annual debt charge of £236,654. The Belgian Government, as one of its first acts in taking over the colony from Leopold, raised a loan of £1,340,671, to be serviced and repaid by the Congo itself. It was to be spent, *inter alia*, for the following purposes:

* This point is elaborated in the next chapter.
† E. D. Morel. *The Future of the Congo*, 1909.

Various enterprises connected in part with
    organizing the Belgian occupation of the
    Katanga   £958,182
Purchase of a battery for the Fort below Boma;
    purchase of artillery, arms, and ammunition   £80,000
Subsidy to King Leopold   £132,000

Morel's petition complained that Belgium also expected the natives to pay £8,944 for the upkeep of a Museum at Tervuren in Belgium, and £2,740 for the upkeep of the Colonial Institute.

The Colonial Minister's budgetary estimates for 1910 required that the natives of the colony also find the following sums:

Annuity to Prince Albert until he succeeds to
    the Belgian throne   £4,800
Annuity to Princess Clementine until she
    marries   £3,000
Annuities to the former officials of the Crown
    domain   £2,400
Annuities to the congregation of the mission-
    aries of Scheut   £2,600
Upkeep of tropical greenhouses and colonial
    collections at Laeken in Belgium   £16,000

'I would merely observe', added Morel, 'that the Belgian Government, alone among the governments of Christendom, claims the right to govern a tropical dependency in Africa by means of enormous taxes wrung from its inhabitants, and by the issue of loans the interest upon which it expects its African subjects to pay; and caps this claim by demanding of these same African subjects that they shall provide subsidies for the Belgian heir apparent and his sister, for ex-officials, for missionary, medical, and philanthropic institutions in Belgium; that they shall provide for the upkeep of museums, institutes, and tropical greenhouses in Belgium, and that they shall even pay the salaries of the governing body of the Congo in Brussels, and the cost of newspapers and periodicals presumably intended for the edification of the members of that body. . . .'

AGREEMENT ON PAPER

The conference ended on 20 February. There was a cheerful reception at the Palace. Only Joseph Kasavubu stayed away. No other leader – Belgian or Congolese – gave the least sign of anxiety about the future. The Prime Minister, M. Eyskens, proclaimed: 'The task has been accomplished . . . I can fearlessly assert in an atmosphere of mutual trust and confidence, almost without parallel in history.' The King recalled the memory of Leopold II. 'An exceptional and admirable factor is that my great-great-uncle did not achieve this union through conquest, but essentially by peaceful methods. . . .'

Lumumba's speech was brimful of goodwill for the Belgians and for the Europeans living in the Congo. 'It is with their collaboration that we wish to create the Congolese nation, in which all will find their share of happiness and satisfaction.' Even Tshombe was happy; he welcomed the proposal to avoid decentralization in the new State. 'Thanks to this basic reform, the independent Congo of tomorrow will escape the dislocation which threatened it.' He was to be the first to retreat from the Brussels agreement.

The final agreement left a great deal unsaid and undone. Economic and other guarantees were to be worked out at a later conference. The constitution itself was left vague, with no clear-cut decision on whether it would be a federal or a unitary state. All that was laid down was the division of functions between the centre and the provinces, with a partition of authority between them.

BELGIAN POLICY ON THE CONGO'S INTEGRITY

The Round Table Conference laid it down that the Congo should achieve its independence 'within its present frontiers'. In the light of the subsequent controversy over Katanga's bid for independence it is important to recall Belgium's policy on the integrity of the Congo. During their rule the Belgians naturally argued that there could be no question of any of the six provinces seceding. This attitude was stated, time and again, with special reference to the separatist tendencies in the Lower Congo.

But it was defined quite specifically, too, in regard to Katanga in the closing stages of the Brussels conference. Two international events had occurred to provoke the Belgians. The French Government – for no reason explained at the time or since – informed the Belgian Ambassador verbally in Paris that France's preferential right to the Congo subsisted and would continue to subsist. This was a reference to an agreement harking back to the bad old days of the Berlin conference of 1884 when Leopold's International African Association promised to grant France a preferential right in the event that, owing to unforeseen circumstances, the Association should be unable to exercise its rights.

The other incident was caused by a deliberately incautious interview granted by the Prime Minister of the Central African Federation, Sir Roy Welensky, in which he said: 'A vast and rich part of Belgian Congo, that will become independent on 1 July, could throw off its old ties and join the Federation. . . .'

The Belgian Government was understandably angered by both these vulture-like attacks on the still hot carcass of the Congo. To the French, the Prime Minister replied with some heat: 'In 1884 it was possible to envisage cessions which were either gratuitous or at a heavy cost. . . . Today, territories and peoples are no longer property which may be a matter for international commerce.' To Sir Roy Welensky he was equally severe. 'First King Leopold II and then Belgium ensured Congolese unity. . . . The Belgian Government protests against suggestions which tend to demolish the work of three-quarters of a century; suggestions that are prompted by motives that are irrelevant to the good of the Congolese people. . . .' He then went on to recall Resolution 2 of the Round Table Conference laying down that 'the Congo State shall constitute on 30 June 1960 six provinces having the geographical configuration of the provinces now in existence.'

Little did the Belgian Prime Minister realize that within a few months his own Government would itself be under heavy pressure, and sorely tempted to dismember the Congo.

Chapter 9

SIX MONTHS TO INDEPENDENCE

*' During my visit I was struck by the splendid vitality
of the native and European population, their stout
faith in the future, their almost unanimous desire for
a wholehearted collaboration with Belgium. I shall
cherish the memory of how they touchingly manifested their attachment to the dynasty.'*

KING BAUDOUIN, January 1960

FOR the Belgians, the penultimate disaster was the complete
breakdown of their relations with the Congo's most influential
leaders during the six months' transition period to independence.
Everything in this crucial period depended on confidence between
the new rulers of the Congo and the Belgians. What went wrong
is easier to describe than to explain.

The Congolese leaders had returned from Brussels elated by
their victory over the Belgians, and bursting to compete for the
political heritage that would come to the winner of the first
national elections set for June 1960. In preparing for the elections
the Belgian Administration continued to behave as if it still
could (and unquestionably should) control events. The habit of
paternalism died hard with them.

There was no question of rigging the elections; but there were
plenty of opportunities to show favour and to help – by financial
subventions and in other ways – the 'pro-Belgian' leaders. Kasavubu was, to start with, still the principal enemy. The favourites
were the old familiar PNP led by Paul Bolya, and the Parti de
l'Unité National Africaine (PUNA) led by Jean Bolikango. The
close second favourites were Lumumba's MNC and its extensive
network of allies.

The great need was funds for campaigning. The task of organizing parties on a nation-wide basis, or through coalitions with
other parties, required considerable sums of money. It was forthcoming in liberal quantities. The Belgians, through convenient

unofficial sources and through industrialists, supplied funds to
PNP, PUNA, and to MNC. The last group obtained additional
sums through the All-African People's Conference in Accra, and
through the Afro-Asian Solidarity Movement in Conakry. But
if the providers of funds imagined they could call the tune, they
were soon to be disillusioned. Patrice Lumumba, for one,
showed his independence of mind. When I saw him in Leopoldville in March 1960, he was still riding high in the favour of the
Belgians; by May he was being openly denounced by officials as
'nothing better than another Hitler'. He had become the Bad
African. Kasavubu was restored to the Belgians' good books;
the bitter attacks of the past were forgotten, and he was praised
for his moderation and integrity. But Kasavubu himself remained
suspicious and unforgiving. He was acting as Minister of Finance
in the interim Government when I saw him in his Leopoldville
office at the end of March 1960. I had enlisted the services of a
Belgian journalist to act as interpreter, but Kasavubu refused to
be interviewed in his presence. His suspicions of the Belgians
went deep; at the same time he retained his faith in Professor
van Bilsen and in other trusty Jesuit friends.

FEDERALISTS *v.* UNITARIANS

My interview with Kasavubu, and a subsequent talk I had with
Lumumba at this time, pinpointed the growing crisis between
the federalists and the unitarians. 'Everybody,' Kasavubu began,
'is trying to isolate Abako. The other leaders don't seem to see
the dangers in trying to isolate us. The Administration is also
pushing in that direction. They imagine that it is possible to rule
the country against the Abako *bloc*. This is a dangerous mis-
calculation. Without the struggle of the Bakongo there would have
been no independence yet. No other part of the Congo has done
as much for it. In forgetting all this the other leaders deceive
themselves, if they imagine they can rule the country without
or against the Bakongo. We can stand alone; the others cannot.'

Kasavubu firmly denied that Abako was purely a tribal
party. 'That it is a national party is shown by its struggle for the
independence of the whole country. We have allies in Katanga,
and to some extent also in Kasai and Kivu. All over the country

there is a growing tendency in favour of our policy of federalism. People will gradually come to see that federalism is a better policy. Tribal conflicts are a result of colonialism. It was a policy of the colonialists to divide and rule, not only of the Belgians. The difference here is that people were not educated to govern themselves. People outside the Congo should know that these people will never again accept colonial rule, even if the period of decolonization should lead to tribal wars and bloodshed. In the immediate future all depends on the Belgians.'

Kasavubu was more anxious about what might happen before independence than afterwards; but he did not rule out the possibility of things going wrong. 'If things should go wrong,' he said, 'we will find ways of dealing with the situation.' I asked him: 'What if the Government of independence should reject your ideas of federalism?' His answer was: 'If it came to a clash we would try to live on our own in the Lower Congo. We would then have to start all over again trying to unite the country on a federal basis, beginning from the bottom. That is the only way unity can be achieved.'

The mood of Patrice Lumumba – harried by visitors in the Leopoldville Headquarters of the MNC as he had been in room 53 of the Cosmopolitan Hotel in Brussels – was in complete contrast to that of Joseph Kasavubu. 'I am very satisfied', he said, 'with what is happening now. There is a good spirit between the Belgians and the Congolese. We know the Congolese are not sufficiently prepared to experience sovereignty. The Belgians know it too. But I am delighted with the Belgian spirit. Now white and black can help each other to build up the country, with each playing his proper role. We must embark on the acceleration of Africanization with the Belgians in the role of technicians. The MNC was the first party to refuse to cooperate with the Administration, but in view of the changed circumstances it is also the first to cooperate with them again.' This statement by Lumumba three months before independence shows how benignly he could feel towards the Belgians when he was confident. His anxieties at that time were about the federalists. 'Our future lies in unity, but the federalists want to organize tribal feuds because they have no support on a national plane. There is no question of my being anti-Kasavubu. He is my personal friend. We fought together against colonialism. Because we fought the colonialists there is no reason for us to establish a dictatorship as the Abako is doing in the Lower Congo, otherwise we would be doing simply what the colonialists did.' He gave many instances of the way in which the Abako were setting up a state within a state in the Lower Congo. I read over to him the notes of my talk with Kasavubu. He responded immediately. 'I suffered more for the cause of independence than he did. I went to prison. Because I say that we want cooperation with the Belgians, I am accused of being bought by the Administration. It is simply not true. The situation has obviously changed, and there is no longer any reason why we should not cooperate with the Administration in the transition period.' I pressed the point about Kasavubu's threat of separation if he did not get his way over federation. 'If Kasavubu does that, then we are in for a bad time. But he will find that we are not the Belgians. We won't be frightened by him.'

The significance of these and other talks I had in Leopoldville in March 1960 is in the cooperative spirit and sense of responsibility shown by Patrice Lumumba. Secondly, nobody was then taking Moise Tshombe seriously; neither the Administration, nor the Congolese leaders. He was treated by everybody as a rather pretentious fop. The real leader of federalism, and the danger to unity, was Joseph Kasavubu.

BELGIAN QUARRELS

It is difficult to determine precisely the grounds for Lumumba's quarrel with the Belgians in April and May 1960. Some say it had to do with financial affairs; others say it was because of Lumumba's intransigence and erratic behaviour – which is not difficult to believe. On the other side it is said that the Belgians, having found Lumumba in a cooperative mood, were angered by his refusal to take their advice. So much was happening in those critical, confusing months that it is impossible to say just what went wrong. The essential point is that Lumumba and the Belgians fell out, and the estrangement – though not yet irrevocably final – directly contributed to the disaster that was soon to follow. The Belgians recalled their High Commissioner, and put

M. Walter Ganshof van der Meersch in control as Minister for General Affairs in Africa. The Minister's reputation was that of Belgium's 'strong man'. His appointment aroused controversy in Brussels and evoked the hostility and suspicions of the Congolese leaders.

Tension was mounting inside the Congo. The *colons* were worried about their position; those who could afford it were sending their families abroad until the uncertainties passed; there was increasing anti-white feeling. The politicians were engaged in political bargaining. In many parts of the country the situation recalled the 'rotten boroughs' of England in the last century. Powerful local chiefs and 'favourite sons' controlled large blocks of votes; their support was strenuously competed for. The battle of the hustings was not yet a feature of Congo politics, although in the larger centres the *évolués* by no means voted tribally. They based their decision either on principle, or on the possible advantages of going with the winning side. But nobody could say with any certainty in this maiden election who was going to win. It was like staking a bet on a card of dark horses.

Contrary to expectation there had been relatively little inter-tribal fighting. The worst incidents continued to occur in Kasai between the Lulua and the Baluba. But nasty as these incidents always are, they were much less severe than had been predicted.

Apart from politics, the factor that should have given most cause for alarm was the financial position of the Congo and its future economic relations with Belgium. But if the Belgians were prepared to take this seriously, the Congolese attitude was that financial questions must await the outcome of the elections. Most of the political parties chose to field only their 'second elevens' at what should have been a decisive conference to settle economic questions in Brussels.

HARD BARGAINING

If the Belgians had shown themselves generous in their final decision to concede independence, they appeared much less so in their financial negotiations with the Congolese leaders. The voice of the *Bourse* was unmistakable.

It is a matter for argument whether the Congo's economy was, in fact, basically sound under Belgian rule. Economists differ strongly. The size of the Public Debt, and the terms under which it was arranged, was alarming. It could be justified only if it were unmistakably clear that the capital raised was being used to develop the country's resources on a basis that allowed for balanced development. There is evidence to show that the economy was in fact lop-sided, when viewed from Leopoldville rather than from Brussels. An expensive European type of economic superstructure had been raised on a pathetically under-developed rural economy. It is possible to argue that this was the quickest way of getting the steam behind an expansionist economy; it is the method adopted by the Russians and the People's Republics. Marxist criticisms, therefore, would be out of place in the Belgian Congo. One would have to judge Belgian policy by the principles of economic planning formulated by under-developed African and Asian states after they had achieved independence. By these standards the Congo was in an unhealthy state.

The constructive feature of the economy was the increase in national revenue at the rate of 4·7 per cent per annum since 1920; between 1950 and 1958 it achieved the impressive rate of 7·6 per cent. Salaried workers had increased rapidly: 1,100,000 (about 40 per cent of the adult male population) were in paid employment. But the national income level was depressingly low; an average of less than eleven shillings per year. The rate of economic growth was not keeping up with the population growth; the population was expected to grow from 13 millions to 27 millions in thirty years. Moreover, the Congo had the unenviable reputation of being the heaviest-taxed country in Africa.

The Congo's economic growth was at the point where a vast expansion of national revenue was needed to maintain its impetus. The Belgian estimate put it at 5 per cent per annum; this called for about £63 million of public investment, plus £91 million of private capital in the five-year period from 1960 to 1965. As against this £154 millions in five years, all the Belgians had managed by way of private and public capital in the period of eight years between 1950 to 1958 was a total of £168 million; and this figure was intended to achieve a lower rate of development than the Belgian experts calculated was necessary for the Congo's future growth.

But if the long-term problems were serious, the immediate economic problems were critical. On the eve of its independence the Government was faced with large current deficits (£40 million on current account for 1960 alone). The flight of capital and the loss of international confidence, because of the events of 1959, meant the new Government would come to power with no liquid assets at all;* a quarter of its budget was already mortgaged to its Public Debt; a portion of its future earnings was drawn upon to repay the advance borrowings in taxes and duties from the principal mining and industrial tax-payers; and, worst of all, it would have little independent control over its own Central Bank.

The Congo Central Bank had been made a prisoner of Brussels early in 1960. The story is a dismal one. Having failed to take any steps to arrest the flight of capital, the Belgians were finally forced to act when the Congo Central Bank reached the point where it could not meet its obligations. Its reserves had been allowed to run down too far. To prop it up, the Belgian National Bank agreed to guarantee its operations on two conditions. First, that its gold and dollar reserves amounting to nearly £15 million in gold and £11 million in convertible sterling should be lodged in the vaults of the National Bank in Brussels. (These assets were removed by the Belgians only after independence; hence the accusation of 'robbery'.) Secondly, that the monetary and public investment policy of the Congo should be settled between the two banks. This meant that the independent Congo would be deprived of a large measure of economic freedom of action. It is astounding that the Belgians should have imagined that such a policy could survive independence.

Belgian lack of understanding was manifested equally in other aspects of their economic dealings with the Congolese. On the one hand they generously offered to pay one-third of the salaries of all Belgian colonial servants who remained on after independence, and to provide an extensive technical aid programme. But

* To help meet this position the Belgians had offered to subsidize the 1960 Budget by £17·5 million; it had raised a long-term loan from the International Bank of Reconstruction for £14 million, and a short-term loan in New York for £7 million. Apart from the economic unwisdom of meeting current and past deficits by long-term loans, the total amount raised in subsidies and loans amounted to less than two-thirds of the estimated 1960 Budget deficit.

these services were to be controlled by a separate department operating under the control of the Belgian Embassy. The normal practice of international aid, based on a Government-to-Government relationship, was repudiated. The civil servants and technical services within the Congo would fall under the control and supervision of the Belgian Government. Here was the last stronghold of paternalism.

None of these basic problems was reflected in the hundreds of resolutions and recommendations finally adopted by the Economic Conference held in Brussels from April to May 1960. The Congolese delegates were unsure of their powers and even less sure of their economics, a fact referred to by the Belgian Prime Minister in his opening address to the conference: 'There are doubtless some persons who fear that in a relatively short period they cannot learn enough about the manifold aspects of the situation. ... Others may fear that Belgium will attempt to impose indirectly some hold over the future Congolese Government through economic, financial, and monetary agreements. There is also some anxiety among the Belgians. Many of our fellow-citizens have families in the Congo whose future appears uncertain. We are aware that the security of the Congo's economic sub-structure – to which the Belgian economy has made heavy sacrifices – could be endangered if fundamental mistakes were made.'

These mistakes were made; but before the enormity of the economic mistakes had been realized by the Congolese, they were overtaken by the consequences of political mistakes which destroyed any possibility of implementing the plans for a Belgo-Congo Economic Community.

Chapter 10

LEADERS AND IDEAS

*'The blacks are still in their infancy as a people.
They may never even attain manhood. . . . If they
ever do attain an equality with white men, it will be the
greatest human triumph in the history of the world.'*
DEMETRIUS C. BOULGER, *The Congo State* (1898)

THE independence election in June 1960, was the first test of
public opinion ever made in the Congo. Its result* was indecisive,
except in one respect. The pro-Belgian parties, like PNP and PUNA,
failed badly, winning between them fewer than one-sixth of the
seats. Apart from Katanga, where Moise Tshombe's CONAKAT
cartel won just over half the seats to beat the BALUBAKAT into
second place, the nationalists won comfortably; but among them
there was no clear victory for either the militant or moderate
wings. And although Patrice Lumumba's MNC emerged as the
largest party, with thirty-three seats in a Parliament of 137 (later
it grew to forty), their strength gave them little more than a strong
bargaining position.

What type of men were these leaders who had suddenly emerged
from the shadows in the wings to crowd the centre of the
stage, which had been held for the best part of a century by the
Belgians?

PATRICE LUMUMBA

The Congo's first Prime Minister, thirty-five-year-old Patrice
Lumumba, typifies what was best and worst in Belgian colonial

* The MNC won seats in each of the six provinces, but had virtually no
support in Leopoldville Province itself. Their main strength lay in Lumumba's own province of Orientale; their allies won strong support in
Kivu (mainly Kashamura's CEREA party), in Katanga (Jason Sendwe's
BALUBAKAT), and in Kasai (the Lulua Frères). The Lower Congo went
solidly to Abako. Between them, Abako and PSA control twenty-five of
the twenty-six seats in Leopoldville Province.

rule. He is a rake of a man, with a tiny, narrow head and a chinful of beard. His smile is light and quick and frequent; when he is angry or frustrated it disappears behind a hard, hostile, impregnable shield. His movements are sharp and wary, like those of a praying mantis. His tongue is silver and seldom still. He thinks nothing of talking for four hours at a time. But his pleasant, easy manner is deceptive; he is earnest and tough, and can be ruthless, as occasion has shown. His hero is Dr Kwame Nkrumah, and the model for his state is Ghana. 'In a young state', he believes, 'you must have strong and visible powers'.

He is a republican and a reformer. 'Our need is to democratize all our institutions. We must separate the Church from the State. We must take away all power from the traditional chiefs, and remove all privileges. We must adapt socialism to African realities. Amelioration of the conditions of life is the only true meaning independence can have.'

His outlook at first was pro-Western. 'Mistakes have been made in Africa in the past, but we are now ready to work with the powers which have been in Africa to create a powerful new bloc,' he said at the beginning of 1960. 'If this effort fails, it will be through the faults of the West.'

His resentment of authority (even of such formidable authority as the United Nations) is what one might have expected from the political heir of the Belgians' great father-figure, King Leopold II. About a great many important things Lumumba is neutral, indifferent, or indecisive, rather than rebellious. It is only when he suspects paternalism that he rebels without thought of the consequences; time and again in the gravest days of the crisis this emotion flared up with a terrifying passion. Paternalism acts on him like an allergy.

On the other hand, his reaction to the Belgian attempt to enforce Christianity on the Congolese is tepid. Having been subjected to both Catholic and Protestant mission influence, Lumumba feels indifferent to both. Yet he is neither an atheist nor anti-Christian. His parents are devout Catholics. His background was by no means wholly hostile to his future, but it put curbs on his ambitions. Submission could get him some way, but not as far as he wished to go: rebellion was more rewarding, and less wounding to his pride. Lumumba's long, lonely rise to the top taught him never wholly to trust. This attitude is reflected in the super-suspiciousness with which he was to look beneath every UN helmet for a potential enemy. His erratic behaviour can be both irritating and disconcerting, but it has the advantage of flexibility. Lumumba's last word is always his first. He must never be judged by his impromptu utterances; these only reflect his passing emotions. He has shown himself to be inflexible only on one important issue: the need for a strong central government.

In the dangerous months after independence Lumumba faced a situation which would have tried the most experienced of statesmen. Recall for a moment the state of the Congo in June 1960, and the difficulties in which he found himself. The Government itself was an uneasy coalition. At first, the civil service was manned entirely by Belgians; later there was no civil service at all, except what was scratched together by the UN. The writ of the Government ran hazardously. Rebellion, when it came through the Force Publique, affected an area the size of Western Europe. Is it altogether surprising that in this cataclysmic situation the young, untried Prime Minister should have appeared impetuous, unreliable, hostile, irresponsible, and, at times, alarming?

Lumumba's mistakes were due partly to his mercurial personality, partly to his one fixed idea – belief in the unitary state – and partly to his inexperience. The victims of this inexperience were also its authors – the Belgians. Until he became Prime Minister, Lumumba's career offered him few opportunities. He had organized a village post office; because of his lack of interest in it he was lax and, so he says, the staff defaulted with the cash; Lumumba went to prison. Next he was given the opportunity to serve as a director of a brewery. Finally, for less than two years he forced his right to organize a political movement. None of these experiences prepared him for the job of running a highly complex country; in the past that job had been exclusively reserved for Belgians. Lumumba was never, perhaps, indispensable as Prime Minister. Nevertheless, he was the only Congolese leader with anything like a national following; a point too often overlooked. Despite his wilder utterances he succeeded in the early difficult months in maintaining, with only a few defections, the solidarity of his widely disparate coalition government. This was no small achievement.

The struggle between unitarians and federalists divides national-

ists throughout Africa. Lumumba belongs to the company of Dr
Nkrumah, Julius Nyerere in Tanganyika, Tom Mboya in Kenya,
and Sékou Touré; all these leaders believe that the only way of
building an effective modern state free from the shackles of narrow
tribal loyalties is to create a single, strong, central government.
Lumumba staked·his career on this firmly held belief. His analysis
was logical, but it failed to take account of all the factors in the
Congo situation. Tribalism, he argued, is divisive, feudal, and out-
dated; the need is to create a single Congolese loyalty; this can be
achieved only through nationalism; its instrument is the visibly
strong central government. But faced with bitter opposition, was
he wise to refuse to compromise in the early days of the life of the
Republic? He argued his case at the Round Table Conference that
gave the Congo its independence in January 1960. He laid it before
the electorate in June 1960, and won an indecisive victory. Finally,
he tried to force it on his federalist opponents when he took control of the first independent Government.

So far, the unitarians have won almost everywhere. They failed
only in Nigeria. Experience may yet show that federalism is the
only way to build viable societies in the larger African countries.
In size and diversity of cultures and development, the Congo has
much more in common with Nigeria than with Ghana. Lumumba's great political error is that he tried to cast the Congo into the
tight mould of Ghana, rather than into the larger, more accommodating mould of Nigeria.

Lumumba's behaviour is not very different from that of nationalist leaders elsewhere; their attitudes are a direct reflection of their
situation. When things are going well they are naturally buoyant,
tolerant, and full of goodwill (see Lumumba's views at the time of
the Round Table Conference and again in March 1960, in Leopoldville). Under pressure they turn inwards, behave suspiciously,
criticize fiercely, and their defiance knows no reason. Lumumba
can be generous, cooperative, and forgiving; and he can be bitter,
destructive, and irrational. This latter mood characterized his behaviour in the months after independence.

JOSEPH KASAVUBU

Joseph Kasavubu, the 50-year-old first President of the Congo

T – E

Republic, had never been out of the Congo before 1959 (except to visit Brazzaville on the other side of the river from Leopoldville). By then he had already clearly formulated his ideas on independence and on federalism. He stands in the same tradition as the leaders of the Western Region of Nigeria. Without ever having read any of his writings or speeches, Kasavubu had come to the same conclusions as Chief Obafemi Awolowo, the first Prime Minister of Western Region and the present leader of the Opposition in the Nigerian Federal Parliament.

It is not entirely surprising that such similar viewpoints should arise independently in Africa; they represent a typical reaction to the challenge of welding powerful tribal states into a modern nation-state. Awolowo's path to Nigerian freedom had as its starting-point the culture and political organization of the Yoruba. He argued that the first essential for Nigerian unity was to entrench Yoruba interests in the Western Region; only afterwards was he prepared to consider a wider Nigerian Federation.

Kasavubu's starting-point was the Bakongo tribe of the Lower Congo. Between the fourteenth and sixteenth centuries, they had formed part of a powerful kingdom, but their fortunes had declined long before the tribe was divided by colonial boundaries between the French Congo, Portuguese Angola, and the Belgian Congo. When Kasavubu first dreamed of reuniting the three parts of the Bakongo, and of recreating his ancient Kingdom, there was not the slightest possibility of the Congo's independence. He believed it would be easier to work for a separate Lower Congo. This was the origin of his policy of separatism, which was converted into federalism when the prospect of Congo independence opened up in 1959, largely through his own efforts. But he never entirely gave up his separatist ideas. His policies alternated unpredictably between a Bakongo Kingdom outside the Congo Republic, and one within a federal Congo state.

Joseph Kasavubu's passionate Bakongo patriotism might perhaps be his way of compensating for not being pure Bakongo himself. His grandfather was a Chinese labourer who had worked on the Congo railway construction; his mother was Bakongo. His mixed ancestry shows in his squat, mongoloid face. He is suspicious, unforthcoming, serious. The lighter side of his personality shows only when he is in the company of trusted friends. He was trained by the Roman Catholics and remains close to the Church. But he is at the same time close to the Bakongo's tribal religionists, the Kibanguists. One of his closest political advisors is Professor A. J. J. van Bilsen, a Belgian liberal and staunch Catholic. He is a Thomist. As a student, the young Kasavubu read classics and philosophy. He was thirty before he finished his studies. The next sixteen years found him working conscientiously in the Treasury Department by day, and engaging in *évolué* society affairs by night, until in 1957 he was elected mayor of Dendale, one of the townships of Leopoldville. He was highly regarded by the Belgians as one of the 'trusties' in the rising *élite* of Congolese. He allowed himself to be 'immatriculated' into the Congo's upper strata, a step refused by many of the political leaders.

Kasavubu is essentially conservative and middle-class. He plods where Lumumba leaps; he ponders where Lumumba rushes into speech. But he is as tough and stubborn as Lumumba. This obduracy and an unrelenting suspicion of the Belgians are the only features the first President and Prime Minister have in common. They formed an indispensable team at the birth of the new Republic. But their alliance was one of expediency; their attitudes are diametrically opposed to each other.

MOISE TSHOMBE

The 'villain' of the Congo drama was always the odd man out among the rising generation of Congolese leaders. Tshombe, the forty-two-year-old leader of CONAKAT (Confederation of the Association of Tribes of Katanga) was never part of the nationalist movement. In the days of colonialism he stuck close to the Belgians, and had he been as good a businessman as his father (who left him a string of businesses) he would have prospered. But he lost his patrimony and went bankrupt three times. However, he never stayed down for long. Like many unsuccessful businessmen he became a leading figure in the politics of commerce: he was President of the African Chamber of Commerce Association.

Tshombe has the bounce of an indiarubber ball, and the facility to leap on any likely-looking bandwaggon. His attempt to seize power in Katanga was an act partly of reckless opportunism, partly of conviction. Had it not been for the active support and flattery of certain Belgian financial circles and *colons* in Katanga, he would never have risked such a daring *coup*. Nevertheless, it is too easy to dismiss Tshombe simply as a stooge of the Belgians. He is certainly an opportunist. At the Brussels conference in January 1960, when the Congo was granted its independence, he expressed himself completely satisfied with the draft constitution, although it did not envisage federation. After the independence elections he negotiated with Patrice Lumumba terms for entering a coalition government without specifying any conditions for a federal constitution. Those negotiations broke down only after Tshombe's impossibly high demands for seats in the Cabinet were turned down. He then raised the banner of Katanga's independence. In the year before independence he had outdone the Belgians in his denunciations of Kasavubu; in the independence elections he formed an electoral alliance with him.

He has consistently used the Belgians for his own purposes; that these purposes happened, at times, to suit the interests of certain Belgians was a coincidence. Tshombe was not always well regarded by the Belgians. At the Brussels Round Table Conference the Government treated him coldly because of his intrigues with financial circles of whom they disapproved. At the first sign of Tshombe's plan to tear Katanga away from the Congo, it was the Belgians who publicly slapped him down. It was only after the revolt of the Force Publique that he won Belgian approval. But his great bid to win Belgian recognition for an independent state of Katanga failed.

Despite his opportunism, his foppish elegance, and his suave manner, Tshombe is not a politician of straw; the mistake made by his opponents was to treat him as one. He is related to the royal family of the Lunda tribe, which is powerful in Katanga and across the border in Northern Rhodesia; his wife is the daughter of the Paramount Chief. He received a good education at American Methodist schools, and he is a formidable tactician. Like Senator McCarthy, he is not afraid to use the smear campaign on his opponents; at one time or another he has accused all his opponents of being Russian agents. It is a line that goes over well in certain Belgian, American, and British circles. But it cuts little ice in the Congo.

Tshombe has been accused of wanting to link Katanga with the

Central African Federation; this is untrue. Some of his Belgian advisers sounded out this idea with Sir Roy Welensky, but it was promptly repudiated by him. African nationalist leaders in Northern Rhodesia have viewed his pretensions with considerable sympathy. At one time he had the support of the militant United National Independence Party.

Tshombe is the perfect example of the type of *évolué* Belgian paternalist policy was designed to produce. Had all the *évolués* been Tshombes, the Belgians would have had no difficulty in carrying through their policy of creating, in time, a Belgo-Congolese Community. The tragedy from their point of view was that Tshombe is not typical.

JASON SENDWE

CONAKAT's principal opponent is the BALUBAKAT cartel composed of three tribally-based parties, representing minority tribes. It is associated with Lumumba's MNC. The leader of the cartel is a 43-year-old Baluba, Jason Sendwe. Like Tshombe, he is a Methodist product. He wanted to be a doctor, but as there were no facilities for medical training in the Congo he could do no better than become a medical assistant. His frustration found an outlet in nationalist politics. He is one of the outstanding young leaders, and is thought of as a possible future Prime Minister.

JEAN BOLIKANGO

At fifty-one the leader of PUNA (the Parti Unité Nationale Africaine) stands out as the Congo's prematurely elder statesman. He is a tall, broad, proud, and handsome man; a fervent Catholic and the leader of the Bangala found in Equatoria and in Leopoldville, whose tribal association forms one of the twenty-five moderate parties grouped together in PUNA. To his own people Bolikango is known as the Sage, and sometimes as the Moses. Most of his life was spent in teaching, and many of today's politicians were his students. He is the only Congolese who rose to a senior post in the Administration – Assistant Commissioner-General of Information in the Congo. Later he repudiated the role he played in *Inforcongo* by an unexpectedly sharp denunciation of Belgian propaganda at the Brussels conference. Still he did not forfeit Belgian confidence.

The main political influence in his life has been the Senegalese poet-politician, Léopold Senghor. But he also finds it possible to admire the conservative President of the Ivory Coast, Félix Houphouet-Boigny, for his 'wisdom and calmness'.

His later arrest by Lumumba was as ironic as it was ineffective; at one time he nearly secured the Presidency with the help of Lumumba. On the question of the constitution he at first stood much closer to Lumumba than to Kasavubu.

PAUL BOLYA

Bolikango stands well to the right of Lumumba and Kasavubu, and Bolya stands to the right of Bolikango. He is the leader of PNP (Parti National du Progrès), a coalition of twenty-seven tribal and territorial associations, mainly concentrated in Equator and in Leopoldville. This was the movement on which the Belgians had staked their hopes. Its moderate conservatism and pro-Belgian sympathies were well suited to the policies of Brussels. But PNP was hopelessly defeated in the independence elections, principally because of its pro-Belgian label. Its opponents transscribe PNP as Parti des Nègres Payés.

Bolya has a strikingly unusual face, like a Bayaka mask; it is a surprise when it becomes animated. He has ability and intelligence. His main influence lies with the Mongo tribe. He is a unitarian, but not harshly so. 'There is no reason,' he believes, 'why each tribe should not remain what it is, yet agree to cooperate on a national level. Our aim should be to blend unitarianism with federalism.' His attitude to his own people is one of paternalism; he therefore understood, and never rebelled against, the Belgians.

ANICET KASHAMURA

The thirty-three-year-old Minister of Information is a politician of an entirely different hue. He is a militant socialist. His party, CEREA (Centre de Regroupement Africain), is strongly established in Kivu, an unusually traditionalist province. It is all the more

surprising, therefore, to find that the ideas of its principal spokesman were moulded by Aneurin Bevan's *In Place of Fear*, and by
the writings of the French socialist, Jules Moch. They won him
away from the influence of the White Fathers.

His aim is to build socialism in the Congo. 'The Africans are
natural socialists.' He once made a brief excursion into Eastern
Europe. 'There is good as well as bad in the little I saw; the same
as in the West. We Africans will not throw away anything simply
for the sake of doing so. We will be guided by our own African
past, and take whatever is useful to us from both the West and the
East.'

Kashamura worked as a book-keeper and a journalist, and was
sent to prison for sedition. He believes that socialism can only
come gradually to a country like the Congo. 'We still need the
industrial *cadres*, and we need to form effective labour organizations. Nationalization must come slowly so as not to frighten
away capital.' The Congo's constitution, he believes, should be
neither unitary nor federalist. It should provide for a strong
central government, but with wide autonomy for the provinces.

ALPHONSE NGUVULU

The thirty-eight-year-old leader of the PP (Parti du Peuple), a
small but sophisticated party of townsmen, stands well to the left
even of Kashamura. He is a student of Marxism which, like Sékou
Touré, he believes is capable of being adapted to Africa's special
conditions. The Belgians regard him and his party as avowedly
communist; but this judgement may be premature.

Nguvulu received his political training in the Belgian General
Federation of Labour, in which he was a prominent office-holder.
Originally a unitarian party, the PP now tends to support the
federalists. But it has little influence, although its propaganda is
vigorous and militant.

ANTOINE GIZENGA AND CLEOPHAS KAMITATOE

Although Gizenga and Kamitatoe lead the PSA (Parti Solidaire
Africain), which controls the populous Kwango and Kwilo
regions of Leopoldville, they are bitter rivals. PSA originated

as a federalist party in alliance with the Abako; it now stands for a compromise between a strong centralized state and federalism.

Gizenga came to be regarded as Lumumba's chief deputy in the Cabinet, although their policies are by no means similar. After attending a seminary he spent some time on the staff of the Catholic mission in Leopoldville. He went to Eastern Europe in the middle of 1959, returning shortly before independence with pronounced communist views. But although he gave the impression of being a doctrinaire communist, in private he spoke with the accents of the African Marxism of Sékou Touré rather than that of Moscow.

Cléophas Kamitatoe, the chairman of the Leopoldville Provincial Assembly, is anything but a Marxist. He is a small, well-built, solemn-faced nationalist, who got his training as a commune secretary in the Belgian Administration.

ALBERT KALONJI

Once Lumumba's chief lieutenant, this thirty-one-year-old accountant and former agricultural instructor is now one of his principal opponents. He leads the breakaway wing of the MNC in the Kasai Province, where he speaks for the Baluba tribe. His quarrel with his former leader was over the high degree of centralization in the MNC. But there is now a doctrinal difference as well: Kalonji believes in federalism. He is an earnest Catholic and a leader of exceptional integrity. But the bitterness of the internecine feud drove him to extremes. His attempt to form the separate Diamond State of Kasai was short-lived.

JOSEPH ILEO

The thirty-eight-year-old President of the Senate also belongs to the breakaway MNC, but is at the same time a member of Abako. He is a sturdy individualist, utterly unafraid of speaking his mind. Ileo was educated in philosophy and sociology, and became the editor of *Conscience Africaine*, a Catholic paper which became the first vehicle for open nationalist propaganda in 1956. His attempt to form a rival Government to Lumumba's failed.

THOMAS KANZA AND JUSTIN BOMBOKA

These two young leaders – Kanza leads the Congo delegation at the UN, and Bomboka was the first Foreign Minister – are latter-day products of Belgian policy; they were among the few Congolese who were allowed to continue their studies abroad after the Second World War.

Thomas is the son of Daniel Kanza, formerly Kasavubu's chief lieutenant. With his father and brothers he leads the Abako splinter movement, which broke with Kasavubu at the Brussels conference in January 1960. After taking an economics degree in Belgium, Kanza spent a year at Harvard University in the United States. Subsequently, he worked with the European Community in Brussels.

Bomboka, too, was allowed to take a degree at a Belgian University. Although he held the post of Foreign Minister, his mellow attitudes found little favour with Lumumba in the stormy days after the revolt of the Force Publique. At considerable danger to himself, Bomboka toured Leopoldville saving Belgians from being ill-treated by the mob. He subsequently joined with Ileo in his abortive attempt to form a rival Government, and still later he went with Colonel Mobutu when the army commander set up his Administration of University Students.

Chapter 11

THE DISASTER

'*The individual feelings of vengeance and of grievance are progressively increased; daily the dissatisfaction rises ...*'

> Report of Belgian Parliamentary Commission
> in April 1959, speaking of Black reactions to
> treatment by Whites

'*Acts against human dignity, humiliations, and outrages against the profoundest values of mankind and
the civilized concept of personal integrity have been
the rule, as if the word had gone round that both
men and women should be humiliated to the greatest
possible extent ...*'

> M. MERCHIERS, Minister of Justice in Belgium,
> 28 July 1960, reporting on Black treatment of
> Whites

THE disaster when it finally came, came swiftly and from an unexpected quarter. The Congo's hope for a peaceful transition to
independence lasted less than a week. On 8 July the Force Publique mutinied in Leopoldville; within three days the rot had
spread throughout the Force. But the trouble had already started
on 4 July, the day after the independence festivities ended. In ten
crucial days the Belgians lost the greater part of their seventy
years' work in the Congo, and the Congolese stood in danger of
seeing their freedom torn from their hands. The country was by
no means leaderless; but the leaders were at cross-purposes, and
powerless. Even the mobs had no real power; their rebelliousness
and lust were vindictive and effervescent. They behaved like auto-
mata. The pressure of their passion spent, they lapsed into
insensate bullying and truculence, and waited sullenly for 'the
punishment that never came'.

RIVALS FOR POWER

Seen at this distance it is possible to reconstruct the events that led to the immolation of the Congo's freedom. This chapter opens on 17 June, the day the Congo's first elected parliament met in Leopoldville. Its immediate task was to elect an heir to the Belgian ruler. It took seven days to demonstrate that there were claimants but no proper heir. The heir apparent, Patrice Lumumba, used every wile to make his claim stick. He negotiated with patience and skill to knit together first one coalition then another; but each came unravelled in the hands of parliament. He made a deal with the pro-Belgian parties, accepting Jean Bolikango as President. When this failed he opened negotiations with Moise Tshombe; but the Katanga leader's terms proved to be too high. In the midst of these tortuous negotiations the Belgian Minister, Walter Ganshof van Meersch, made a surprising decision. Without waiting for Lumumba to complete his task of trying to form a Government, he invited Joseph Kasavubu – the only Congolese leader who had refused to negotiate with Lumumba – to take over this responsibility. It was this action that broke the last tenuous link between Lumumba and the Belgians. When Kasavubu's efforts also failed, the two rivals were persuaded by leaders of the African states, including Dr Nkrumah, to patch up their quarrel temporarily. They agreed to share power, with Lumumba as Prime Minister and Kasavubu as President and Commander-in-Chief of the Armed Forces.

It was on this inauspicious note that the Congo celebrated its independence from 30 June to 3 July. The King of the Belgians was there to give his blessing to the new African States, and to recall the beneficence of King Leopold II. Lumumba, still smarting from his treatment at the hands of the last Belgian Governor-General, was pointedly offensive to the royal guest. 'We are no longer your monkeys,' he shouted.* The Force Publique was on hand to deal in its usual clobbering manner with the surging crowds. Nobody then suspected they would be the *deus ex machina* in the final disaster.

The new Government was shaky from the outset. Almost all

---

* 'You monkey' is a term of abuse often used by Belgians. The Congolese felt it a particularly hateful insult.

the parties were represented in the Government, including the pro-Belgian PNP and PUNA, and even a representative of CONAKAT. It was a coalition of rivals, and their rivalry was sharp and principled. They represented opposite views on a wide range of political ideas – the most important, of course, being their attitude to unitarianism or federalism. They agreed to work together because they wished to see the Belgians removed from the saddle of power, and because they feared the country might disintegrate even before it was fully launched on its way to nationhood. Their first task was to work out a constitution, with parliament as a Constituent Assembly.

On 3 July the distinguished visitors packed their bags, leaving the Congo to settle down to its more solemn affairs. Only Dr Ralph Bunche, the United Nations representative, lingered on to see how things would work out. It was just as well he did. The first whiff of trouble came on 4 July; but at the time nobody appears to have paid much attention. At Camp Hardy (near Thysville, between Leopoldville and the sea), members of the Force Publique, armed with long knives, menaced their Belgian officers. 'We are the masters now,' they said. They broke open the armoury and helped themselves to ammunition. The next day was one of critical anxiety, with the Europeans crowded together on a hill in the officers' quarter. Three Belgians, badly beaten, were carried in from outside. It was not until the following day – 6 July – that the position was relieved by a Congolese delegation, later reinforced by President Kasavubu and Premier Lumumba, who came to reason with the troops. They quickly retrieved the position. The Belgian officers considered the trouble ended; for the next three days they carried on as usual. No special precautions appear to have been taken despite their bad fright. Not even the refusal of the Congolese to present themselves for duty from 7 to 10 July struck them as ominous at the time. This attitude is hard to understand in the light of subsequent complaints made by the Belgians and their wives from Camp Hardy. Referring to events from 4 to 10 July, a civilian in Thysville complained he was badly beaten by troops, and brought to the camp; another claimed he and his family had been held prisoners for two days, and that they had been threatened with violence. A Belgian officer, describing the situation in Camp Hardy on 5 July, says that 'the officers were virtually prisoners, and two of them were beaten with sticks and stoned'. Nevertheless, they carried on 'normally' (to quote the official Belgian report on atrocities) until the storm broke in their camp on 11 July.

Meanwhile, there had been incidents in other parts of the country. A Belgian woman claims that on the night of 5 July she was raped sixteen times by Congolese soldiers in her home at Kisantu. On 6 July Belgian civilians were attacked at Inkisi; six women claim they were all victims of unsuccessful rapes; three Belgians were arrested and 'forced to flatten out rolls of barbed wire with our naked feet'. Lower down the Congo, at Banza-Boma, two women claim they were raped by soldiers on 5 and 6 July. A Swiss citizen was arrested by police at Matadi, and severely beaten. 'That's what independence is!' he was told. On 8 July four women and a girl were raped in Matadi by police and soldiers, while several men were arrested. In the Bakongo country there was an unusual feature: white women were forced to cut grass barefoot in the savannah, the only apparent purpose being to humiliate them by forcing them to work as African women worked.

Still there was no official protest, nor any sign of precautions. On 7 July Mr Lumumba was entertained by foreign journalists at the Zoo at Leopoldville; none of the correspondents, Belgian or otherwise, questioned his statement that, despite predictions, no cases of theft or rape had occurred. Lumumba spoke confidently, although trouble was already brewing in the capital. On the previous day, 6 July, members of the Force Publique had tried to force their way into parliament. One of the rebels told a newspaper correspondent that the revolt was not aimed at the Whites but 'at the Belgian officers and some of our rulers'. The trouble had started in the Leopold II Camp, where soldiers met on the night of 5 July to discuss their grievances. They expressed strong resentment against Lumumba's decision to appoint Belgians to national defence posts. The officers who tried to break up the meeting were disobeyed and disarmed. Lumumba at first showed no sympathy with the delegation sent by the men of the Force to discuss their grievances with him on 6 July. He told them firmly that he intended to stand by his appointment of Belgian officers. Dissident elements in the Force reacted more strongly on 7 July when a ministerial car was stoned. Then the Cabinet took a more serious view of what was happening. They decided to break the tension by agreeing to the removal of the Belgian commander of the Force Publique, Lieutenant-General Émile Janssens, and his staff. They also agreed that all Congolese non-commissioned officers should be promoted one rank. But their proposal failed to achieve its purpose.

On 8 July the Force Publique took to mob violence in the capital; policemen led the violence in Matadi; the soldiers broke loose in Sanda in the Lower Congo. Alarmed at the extent and dangers of the violence – with tens of thousands of Belgians fleeing in all directions and reports telling of many thousands held up and threatened in places all over the country – the Belgians decided to fly paratroops to lend protection to their compatriots.

On 9 July the troops mutinied in Kongoloa camp in Katanga; on the same day they overwhelmed and disarmed Belgian officers in the General Gilliard Camp in Luluabourg, the capital of Kasai. On 11 July the Belgian paratroops occupied Leopoldville and dispersed to all parts of the country. Their arrival was the signal for the rebellion to flare up everywhere. The simmering discontent in Camp Hardy at Thysville erupted; the same happened in the Belgian military base at Matadi, and in Stanleyville, the capital of Occidentale. This was also the day Moise Tshombe chose to proclaim the independence of Katanga. His decision, coinciding with the influx of the Belgian Army, broke the camel's back. It was difficult to avoid the impression that the Congo was being taken over by the Belgians and their allies. From then on the tide of violence rose sharply, and the situation deteriorated swiftly. Grievances fastened on rumours, rumours fed suspicions, and suspicions fanned the forces of mutiny and rebellion. The Conference of Independent African States was quick to act. On the initiative of Dr Nkrumah, Lumumba was persuaded to call in the United Nations. The decision was taken on 12 July. From that moment the story took a different turn.

The mutiny changed everything; it destroyed what was hopeful in the situation; it killed cooperation between the Belgians and the Congolese; it splintered the brittle alliances of the Coalition Government; it opened the way for foreign intervention; and it wrecked internal security. Those trained to uphold law and order were themselves the leaders of lawlessness and disorder.

Here was the final irony: the instrument, fashioned by the Belgians at the outset of their occupation of the Congo to establish and maintain their rule, turned in their hands to destroy them. Nobody had foreseen this possibility. On the eve of the mutiny, the Commander of the Force Publique, General Janssens, attended an American July the Fourth party in Leopoldville. Laughing and joking, he met questions about the security position in the Congo with easy confidence: 'The Force Publique? It is my creation. It is absolutely loyal. I have made my dispositions'.*
Three days later he was dismissed; a few days more and the Force Publique had become the rogue elephant of the Congo.

THE FORCE PUBLIQUE

The Force Publique was created by Governor-General Camille Janssen and Baron van Eetvelde in July 1891. Their plan, approved and passed into law by King Leopold II, was to raise twelve companies of Congolese soldiers under the command of 120 European officers. The force was composed of volunteers and levies. Conscription was justified by Baron van Eetvelde in a report he submitted in 1897: 'The State has set itself the task of creating a purely national army, with the view of lightening the budget of the considerable charges which weighed upon it through having to recruit abroad. ... It considers, moreover, the period of military service as a salutary school for the native, where he will learn respect for authority and the obligations of duty.'

The Batetela contingent of the Forces saw their duty in a different light. When their chief, Gongo Lutete, was executed they mutinied in 1895. They killed several Belgian officers, and their revolt was finally crushed with heavy losses. Two years later the Batetela in Baron Dhani's column, advancing towards the Nile to head off the Dervishes, again mutinied. Ten Belgian officers were killed. The mutineers took a French priest, the Rev. Achte, prisoner. When they threatened to kill him he cried out in the local dialect: 'I am a man of God; leave me alone.' This created a diversion in his favour. Some of the mutineers defended him.

* Frank Barber gives this account in *Africa South In Exile*, Vol. 5, No. 1.

Two chiefs addressed him: 'We have killed the Belgians, who called us animals and who killed our chiefs and our brothers as we kill goats. Why should we not kill you?' The priest replied he was not a Belgian; he had never injured the Blacks, he was their true friend. Some of the women began to take his part. At last the principal chief declared: 'I forbid you to kill this white man. Let the man who wishes to kill him take a gun and send a bullet through him. Here he is seated at my side.' Despite this fortunate deliverance the Rev. Achte subsequently described the mutineers as 'indeed terrible savages, eaters of dogs, and some tribes among them also of human flesh ... they have no discipline, no idea of respect for their chiefs'.*

The Force Publique was used to enforce King Leopold's System. Paid an average wage of just over £3 a year, the troops were allowed to live off the land. The Congo Reform Association repeatedly complained of their brutal methods. 'Wherever its operations have ranged native livestock has almost totally disappeared; native preventive measures against the spread of venereal disease have been impossible of application. From far and wide – especially perhaps from Kasai – women have been raided in enormous numbers to satisfy its lusts. ... It is admitted in one official document that "a veritable slave-trade in women" was carried out by them. It was due to the nature of the tasks assigned to this so-called Force Publique under its European officers that the Italian Government finally withdrew its sanction for Italian officers – whose indignant protests were ventilated in the Italian military journals and in the Italian Chamber by Signor Santini – to take service in the Congo.'†

These strictures on the Force Publique largely fell away after the Belgian Parliament assumed control for the affairs of the Congo. But the original concept of Janssen and Baron van Eetvelde remained until the mutiny in 1960: it was still a native army, almost entirely illiterate, poorly paid, and officered entirely by Europeans. It was developed as a dual purpose Force: to defend the frontiers against foreign attack, and to maintain internal security. The Force fought well in two world wars. But in 1944 the non-commissioned officers and troops in Luluabourg mutinied

* Boulger, D. C. *The Congo State.*
† Morel, E. D. *The Future of the Congo.*

and killed a number of Belgian officers. It never flinched, however, when commanded to act against the nationalist movements in the Leopoldville riots and in Stanleyville in 1959. Its strength at independence was 1,006 European officers and 23,000 men. It suffered from two basic weaknesses: the bulk of the men were illiterate, often drawn from the most backward parts of the country, and there was no opportunity for the small *cadre* of educated and trained men to become officers. Before independence several attempts were made to persuade the Commander of the Force to announce plans for Africanizing the army; the result was the selection of a *cadre* of young men to be trained as future officers in Belgium. But up to independence the colour line was rigidly maintained. It was finally broken down with the frightening carelessness of a mindless Frankenstein.

THE PATTERN OF VIOLENCE

Violence in the Congo was of two kinds: the anti-European demonstrations, and the more savage attacks on dissident tribesmen in Kasai, Katanga, and elsewhere. The main sufferers were the Baluba; their special position is discussed in a later chapter.

The evidence produced by the Belgians in their White Paper on atrocities, on 28 July 1960, makes it possible to form some idea of the nature of the violence. Although the Belgians have never given official figures, the estimate of European fatalities is perhaps a score. Raping of women was often accompanied by acts intended to humiliate them. Ill-treatment of men was usually calculated to degrade them. Priests and nuns were singled out in many cases for special insults. The perpetrators of violence were almost entirely soldiers and police; civilians seldom took the initiative in the attacks. In many instances it required the intervention of a single disciplined African non-commissioned officer or a loyal servant to protect Europeans. Those singled out for special acts of revenge were the Flemings, who formed the largest section of the *petits colons;* their behaviour had been specially criticized by the Belgian Parliamentary Commission in their 1959 report.

Despite equivocations Mr Lumumba admitted at a United Nations Press conference that Belgians had been 'molested'.

T – F

Although it is necessary to treat atrocity stories with reserve, it is plain nonsense to pretend the Belgians were not cruelly treated in the mutiny. Reputable foreign correspondents' accounts of what they saw provide sufficient evidence to suggest that some terrible things occurred. It was in the very nature of the situation that the tragedy, once it happened, should be accompanied by vengeful behaviour. But the extent of the atrocities should be kept in perspective; out of a total of 80,000 Belgians in the Congo at independence perhaps one per cent complained of actual ill-treatment.

Until the Congolese establish their own version of what happened, the Belgian White Paper is the only detailed account of the atrocities available. I have selected several passages from the Belgian account to present an impression of the pattern of violence, and to raise some questions.

The Europeans at Sonankulu were thrown into Thysville prison. They were humiliated, stripped naked, people spat in their faces; they were beaten and ridiculed.

At Luluabourg, 1,500 Europeans barricaded themselves into the Immokasai Building where they were besieged ... the siege, with rifle and intermittent machine-gun fire, was maintained until the arrival of the paratroops on the following evening, July 10. Some of those besieged were wounded. ... Families which did not find safety in the Immokasai Building were often the victims of serious outrages. ... A European civilian was shot down. ... Two families, each with several children, were molested and beaten. ... Mrs Z. was raped at gunpoint in her home by two policemen. Both families were then taken to the military camp ... the soldiers told the crowd standing by that their prisoners had shot at them. The crowd went mad. The two mothers were stripped of their clothing, molested, and beaten. They were then locked into the prison. In the presence of her children, a soldier lifted Mrs Z's skirts and pretended to insert a hand grenade in her vagina. The husbands were beaten. ... Mrs Y. was taken out of her house and raped in the road before the eyes of her three children and her husband, who had previously been beaten. Other women, including an old lady were stripped of their clothing, molested, and publicly humiliated.

The total established casualties in this account of what happened in Luluabourg are two women raped, several molested, one man shot, and two families maltreated.

Boende was the terminus of the odyssey of many civil servants. The

Congolese set up road barriers at the suggestion of the Force Publique. ... As soon as they were stopped on the road, the whites were searched ... the men were stripped to the waist, their shoes were removed, and they were roped together. The women and children were separated from the men. ... All were severely beaten with gun butts, fists and kicks; they were spat at and insulted by the soldiers, policemen, and natives. The latter appeared to be urged on by the soldiers. Finally, the soldiers were obliged to protect their prisoners from the native civilians who demanded that the men should be put to torture and the women handed over for their enjoyment. The natives had thus grouped some forty white men, as many women, and at least eight children. Women prisoners were raped in public, often standing up with a child in their arms, surrounded by soldiers, policemen, and civilians, all of whom entered the cells. ... At dawn a party of missionaries from Djolu arrived, also under arrest. Three of them were nuns, their robes in rags, their coifs torn off, all of them ill-treated. ... Men suffering from bullet-wounds were also brought in, a lieutenant ... and a civil servant. A doctor was at first refused permission to care for the lieutenant. Later permission was granted, but as soon as the wound was bandaged, a Congolese soldier wrenched it off again and broke the man's head open above the eyebrow.

The only account in the White Paper that lends itself to analysis is that of the events that occurred in Camp Hardy where, despite the first abortive mutiny, the Belgian officers appear to have been taken by surprise when the troops disarmed them on July 11. According to the official version:

The victims' accounts of the raping resemble a scene from Dante's *Inferno*. The natives attacked all the women, including those obviously pregnant or ill and those who had recently given birth to children. To achieve their aims, the natives used physical violence, the menace of their weapons, and, in innumerable cases, they threatened to kill the children if the mother did not yield. ... Of the twenty-nine white women already questioned, nineteen – or two-thirds of them – acknowledge that they had been raped. ... (One) lady states that to her knowledge nine-tenths of the white women at Camp Hardy underwent the same treatment (that is, they were physically raped).

A week after the 'Inferno' at Camp Hardy, George Clay of the *Observer* arrived there with the UN Force. This is his account:

What began as a mutiny seems to have turned into a leaderless and nervous reaction to the threat of Belgian counter-measures. This view was confirmed by a young Belgian officer, Lieutenant E. Schoonbroodt, who elected to remain at Camp Hardy when the other officers left. He, a Belgian non-commissioned officer, and a doctor and his wife are the only whites still in Camp Hardy. Schoonbroodt contradicted stories of wives of white officers in camp having been raped. He said some gangs of young recruits had run amok in Thysville itself and had raped women and assaulted men there. But when the Congolese NCOs heard of this they did their best to get these troops back under control. The majority of soldiers at Camp Hardy had not got out of hand. Schoonbroodt has remained in camp as 'technical assistant' to the newly-appointed Congolese officers. None of the houses of Belgian officers in the camp had been damaged or looted. Against this appearance of normality, however, must be set the complaints of Congolese civil servants to Colonel Ben Omar (the UN commander) that some Congolese soldiers were still looting in the town – the shops of Congolese businessmen in some instances.

These two accounts, though complementary in some respects, nevertheless present widely different pictures of what happened. The fact that four Belgians, including one woman, voluntarily chose to stay on through the 'Inferno' suggests a different picture from the official version. Equally puzzling is Lieutenant Schoonbroodt's statement that none of the officers' wives had been raped in the Camp itself; a startlingly different version from that suggesting that nine-tenths of the women had been raped. I draw no conclusions from these two versions: neither can be accepted at its face-value.

REASONS FOR THE MUTINY

What is the proper explanation for the revolt of the Force Publique? We are asked to believe two totally different versions about its origins. On the Belgian side there are those who fix responsibility on Lumumba, while on his side the blame is fixed on the Belgians. Can it be that neither was to blame; that the blame is to be found in the total situation that emerged from the tangled past of the Congo?

Why should Lumumba have wished the Force Publique to revolt within days of his own decision to enforce their discipline under Belgian officers? Had he suddenly become afraid of a plot whereby the Force was to be used to kill him and to re-establish

Belgian control? The evidence for this charge is extremely thin. On the first day of the revolt in Leopoldville, the rebels were denouncing Lumumba and demanding the dismissal of their Belgian officers. When he and Kasavubu undertook their mission of pacification, the rebels did not at once rally to their side. They remained fractious and undisciplined.

The charges against the Belgians are equally insubstantial. The Force was the last 'effective' instrument in their hands. Why surrender it? If they had inspired the revolt, how account for the fact that it was immediately turned against themselves? The suggestion is that when the attempt was made to instigate the Force against Lumumba, the Congolese reacted in resentment. But they did not rally to the defence of the Lumumba Government; they put their terms to it, and remained discontented even after their case had been conceded.

The difficulty one faces in trying to understand what happened is that the pattern of revolt was by no means consistent. It had no single head, no obvious goal. The only consistency was the widespread demand for the replacement of their Belgian officers. This might be accounted for on grounds of self-interest. But the final impression is that there was no real loyalty between the men and their officers; not perhaps a surprising discovery in a 'colour bar' army. The members of the Force had cause for dissatisfaction. They were badly paid, extremely hard-worked, and without status. Their Belgian officers had told them: 'Independence is not for you.' It is not surprising that they should have decided to 'organize' a piece of independence cake for themselves: everywhere Blacks were replacing Whites, why not in the army? But after their claims had been conceded, discipline broke and vengeance followed.

The mutiny was comparatively restricted up to the time the Belgian paratroops arrived. There is not the least doubt that their intervention caused the mutiny to take the turn it did. Paratroops of whatever nationality are never gentle; their behaviour in the Congo was no exception. One of their first acts was to arrest the newly-appointed commander of the Force Publique. In places like Matadi they wantonly destroyed areas of the town after all the Belgians had been evacuated.

It is not easy to criticize the Belgian action in committing their paratroops in the Congo to protect their civilians. Would any nation – European or African – have refused to come to the aid of their compatriots caught up in a dangerous insurrection? That the Belgian motives were misunderstood is not surprising; that the whole enterprise led to greater disaster, and the virtual expulsion of the Belgians from the Congo, is part of the dismal tragedy.

M. TSHOMBE'S KATANGA

The Katanga story is not a tidy one in which one can hope to discover a deep-seated, cunning plot and a simple-minded stooge chosen to lend it verisimilitude. If M. Tshombe was the villain, his role was that of an independent-minded African leader with purposes of his own. It must not be supposed that Tshombe was without a large measure of African support. Criticisms of his role arise from his willingness to rely on doubtful methods and elements to pursue his broad federalist aims. It was this choice of methods and aims that set him apart from the rest of the Congolese federalist leaders.

Tshombe's decision to declare Katanga independent at the height of the mutiny, and to make himself head of the Republic, helped finally to bring the Congo to its knees. Why did he do it? There was always at the back of his mind the idea of creating a special relationship for Katanga with the rest of the Congo. It must have seemed to him on 11 July that the Congo was disintegrating, and that this would be a good moment to try and isolate and insulate Katanga. He had previously made 'noises' in the direction of independence, but, as has been shown in earlier chapters, the Belgians always opposed this aim. *Now they supported him.* They may even have encouraged him; but the initiative was his own. It is easy to see how in that dark hour with all their hopes and plans crumbling, their people fleeing in all directions, and their large investments threatened, the Belgians were tempted to grasp at the last straw offered by Tshombe's gamble. They put Belgian troops at his disposal, and a Belgian took control of the Katanga Army. They ordered civil servants and *colons*, who had fled to neighbouring Northern Rhodesia for security, to return to Katanga under penalty of economic sanctions. They sent high-ranking ambassadors to establish liaison between the Katanga Government and their own. They warned the United Nations to keep their troops out of Katanga, and they began to lobby the Western countries to recognize Katanga's independence. Their diplomatic feelers met with little response; only France was not entirely negative. And despite Tshombe's insistence and his subsequent bitter complaints, the Belgian Government itself withheld such recognition.

It is important to get the record straight on this question of recognition because it came to be widely believed that the Western countries were willing to support Katanga's independence. The African States, uneasily suspicious still of Western policies in Africa, seem to believe this myth. But the facts are otherwise. Neither the United States, nor Britain, nor any of the other Western Powers (except France) was willing even to consider recognizing Tshombe's Katanga. Pressure by three former 'Suez rebel' MPs in Britain met with a completely cold reception. Belgium found herself virtually isolated within the West; this position angered the Belgians so deeply that for a time they behaved like a freshly wounded bull. Their threat to abandon NATO shows their unreasoning anger against their allies.

For a time Tshombe's Katanga looked like an oasis in the Congo; its Government was united; its administration worked; its mining and industrial enterprises continued normally. There was law and order in the capital and, so far as one could tell, throughout the province as well. The only shadow that fell over this idyllic picture was when Tshombe summoned his Provincial Government. The BALUBAKAT leaders stalked from the shadows, denounced Tshombe's 'fantasy government', and returned to their strongholds in the 'bush' pursued by the barbed attacks of Tshombe. Although the Assembly was not summoned again, its one meeting was enough to show that Katanga was by no means solidly behind the Government. This was subsequently made painfully clear when Tshombe's forces – imitating what Lumumba's forces had previously done in Kasai – massacred Baluba tribesmen in the opposition stronghold.

But whatever support there was for Tshombe, his Government involved no more than a dozen people: the President, a few Ministers, a Belgian colonel, and some senior officers, and one or two advisers from the Union Minière*. He spent a great deal of time with the foreign Press, exhorting international opinion through them. He had reckoned to secure Belgian backing to the limit. This support included not only complete recognition for the sovereignty of his state, but also Belgian commitment to resist the UN should they attempt to put their Force into Katanga. In the end the Belgians were compelled to give way; again their mistaken policies resulted in the nails being driven deeper into their tortured body.

Before leaving Tshombe's Katanga to consider its subsequent embroilment with the UN, it is important to consider the deeper problems raised by his attempt to create an independent republic. What is the right attitude to adopt when people in a small territory claim the right to form their own state? Are they entitled to expect the automatic support of liberal-minded people in the international community? It is a question that has frequently arisen in Europe in the past, and latterly also in Asia – for example in the case of the Nagas in India, and the Karens in Burma. There is obviously no golden rule, but in the African context one can clearly see some of the factors that must be taken into account in coming to an equitable decision.

Present-day boundaries in Africa cannot be considered sacrosanct, any more than those in Europe a century ago. They have all been artificially drawn, mostly for the convenience of foreign rulers, and with little regard for ethnological or economic factors. This is, in fact, the thesis of the Pan-Africanists themselves. It is a sensible thesis, especially if it is taken in conjunction with another thesis: that there should be no balkanization in post-colonial Africa. Europeans have had their own experience of the evils of

* Eric Downton, the correspondent of the London *Daily Telegraph* described the situation from Elizabethville in an account published in his paper on 27 July 1960: 'The masquerade of Katanga "independence" is becoming daily more pathetic. M. Tshombe, the self-styled President, is today far more under the domination of Belgian officials than he was as an obscure politician before Congo independence. His regime depends entirely on Belgian arms, men, and money. Without this, his Government would in all probability be quickly pulled down from within and without. The outline of Belgium's emergency policy for Katanga is now discernible. It is to protect the great Belgian financial stake here and to hold a political bridgehead in the hope of a Congolese union amenable to Belgium and the West.'

balkanization, and Africans rightly wish to avoid these evils. Moreover, they have a deep suspicion that some of the departing Colonial powers may wish to leave behind them a continent of small and powerless nations which, though nominally independent, will be as easy to prey on as they were when they were still colonial possessions. This suspicion goes deep, and it finds strengthening confirmation in the events in Katanga.

Does Katanga, a tiny country with a population of fewer than two millions, offer a reasonable basis for an independent state? It will immediately be said that all people should have the automatic right to decide their own future, even if this should lead to a continent of Andorras. To this there are two answers. Firstly, that a decision about the future of a territory should be freely made by all its inhabitants, and that those of their neighbours most likely to be affected by the decision should be consulted. How does Katanga emerge from these two tests? In the 1960 independence elections the people of Katanga voted between two major cartels; both favoured Congo's integrity, with CONAKAT favouring federalism. In the provincial elections CONAKAT won by a narrow margin, with twenty-five seats to BALUBAKAT's twenty-two; the remaining thirteen seats returned candidates who mostly sided with CONAKAT. Whatever story these figures can be made to tell they are hardly a convincing display of an overwhelming desire by the people of Katanga to set up their own State – a question that was never in fact put to them.

Next one must consider the effect on the rest of the Congo, if Katanga seceded. Although it holds only 12 per cent of the country's population it produces more than 60 per cent of its revenue. The effect of stripping it away would be like taking the Ruhr out of Germany, or the Midlands out of Britain. This point needs more careful elaboration.

Africa is basically a poor continent with scattered outcrops of unusual mineral wealth – gold on the Witwatersrand, copper in the Northern Rhodesian Copperbelt, the 'geological monstrosity' of Katanga. It is a natural desire of people living close to sources of wealth to keep it for themselves; one has seen this with the oil-rich sheikdoms in the Persian Gulf, and with other areas of Africa, such as the Ivory Coast and Gabon. The result of allowing a relatively small community to hog a wealthy corner would be to condemn vast areas to rural slumdom or permanent economic subjection. It is one thing for a small country, like Nyasaland, to choose poverty in independence rather than wealth in political servitude; it is quite another for a small wealthy country to exercise the right to keep its pile to itself. Moral questions aside, it must inevitably produce political instability, with the poorer neighbour wishing to lay hands on a share of the wealth. This desire would be strengthened in the case of a country, like Katanga, where a colonial power actively assisted in propping up the secessionist Government.

In the seventy years of their hegemony, the Belgians riveted the unity of the Congo to Katanga. They encouraged migratory labour from other parts of the country. They used the taxes of the Congo to develop the infra-structure of Katanga to make it the only properly developed region in the country. Thus the bulk of the capital works programme was paid for by the Congolese themselves; all the public utilities – transport, electricity, roads – were paid for, and are owned by, the Congo Government – not by the Belgian Government, nor by the present Katanga Provincial Government. Moreover, at least 25 per cent, and possibly much more, of the shares of the mines in Katanga are actually owned by the Congo Government. All this is the property of the Congolese, representing their savings and labour. Finally, the greatest part of the development in Katanga was made possible through public loans secured by the Congo Government. If Katanga stands today as a valuable asset, it is because of the contributions made by the Congo as a whole over generations of slow growth and development. It is an integral part of the economy of the whole country.

To pretend that Katanga is simply a piece of real estate belonging to its present rulers is to ignore these facts. Belgians who try to justify Katanga's secession by stirring reminders of human liberty and rights, ignore their own history as well as their own pledges. As we have seen, throughout the negotiations with the Congolese leaders it was the Belgian Government which insisted as a condition for independence that the integrity of the whole of the Congo should be maintained. The treaty guaranteeing independence sets the frontiers as those of the six provinces. The Belgians themselves undertook to defend those frontiers. The fact that things did not work out smoothly is no justification for tearing up these agreements. Judged by the harsher conditions of political reality it was never possible to see how anybody could imagine that such a State could survive for very long in Africa. It would be a State with the sign of Cain on its brow. It would be marked down for swift reprisal action. There is nothing nice about this reality, but that is no reason for refusing to face it.

THE DIAMOND STATE

Tshombe's example was followed in August 1960 by Albert Kalonji, formerly Lumumba's chief lieutenant and leader of the breakaway MNC. Raising the banner of independence over the Baluba area of Kasai, with Bangwala as its capital, he called it 'The Diamond State'. More than 90 per cent of the diamond potential of the Congo comes from that region.

Kalonji's enterprise ended more disastrously than Tshombe's. Before the end of August Lumumba's forces (supported by those of the Kasai Provincial Government) had invaded Bangwala, put Kalonji and his Ministers to flight, and massacred more than a thousand Baluba.

The difficulties in which the hapless Baluba found themselves need some elaboration. As with many large tribes, the Baluba did not live in one homogeneous land unit. They were concentrated in northern Katanga and eastern Kasai. Though a large, vigorous, and intelligent tribe, they had the misfortune to find themselves in a minority in both provinces. Their tribal-based parties in Katanga (part of the cartel of BALUBAKAT) and in Kasai initially sought security and authority by allying themselves with Lumumba's nation-wide MNC. They realized that it was only by avoiding their isolation as a tribal party that they could hope to escape the danger of being dominated in Kasai and Katanga. But when Kalonji broke with Lumumba* he put the Kasai section of the Baluba into the danger of isolation they had sought to avoid. To reduce the dangers of this isolation he later embraced the loose federalist movement, which brought him into close alliance with Tshombe and Kasavubu, and into further conflict with the dominant tribal party in Kasai (that of the Lulua) which was allied with Lumumba.

* See page 71.

The Katanga Baluba had refused, however, to follow Kalonji when he broke away; their leader, Jason Sendwe, stuck to Lumumba. In Katanga the Baluba were fighting a defensive action against an attempt by the majority tribes, brought together in Tshombe's CONAKAT, to dominate the province. This division put the Baluba tribes in the worst of both worlds. They were massacred in Katanga by Tshombe's 'federalists', in Kasai by Lumumba's 'nationalists'.

Describing the massacre of the Baluba, Hammarskjöld spoke of the crime of genocide – the destruction of an entire race. His motives were undoubtedly right, but the charge of genocide cannot be upheld. The fact that the Baluba were killed in large numbers by opposite armies was not caused by any animosity towards them as a race. There was no policy to kill them off as a tribe; nor do the number of fatalities, high as they were – probably 3,000 – justify the charge of genocide. The tragedy of the Baluba is that the wheel of political roulette spun against them in both provinces; their leadership was incapable either of foreseeing their mortal weakness or, if they had seen it, of doing anything about it. The subsequent action of Kalonji in trying to set up his 'Diamond State' – although he had no possibility of defending it from attack – was the culminating error in a series of costly errors for the Baluba. But this is not the end of the story. The pendulum is still swinging violently in the Congo; if it should favour the Baluba, as yet it might, there will be heavy reprisals unless security is firmly established before that day comes.

Chapter 12

INTERNATIONAL DECISION

*'The natives are not represented at this conference
... nevertheless the decision of this body will be of
the gravest importance to them.'*

SIR EDWARD MALET, Britain's representative
at the Berlin conference on Africa, 1885

*'There should not be any hesitation, because we are
at a turn of the road where our attitude will be of
decisive significance, I believe, not only for the future
of the United Nations Organization but also for the
future of Africa. And Africa may well in present circumstances mean the world.'*

MR DAG HAMMARSKJÖLD, addressing the Security Council, 22 July 1960

*'In the United Nations lies the only hope for the
future of all nations. We should all of us, therefore, be
most careful not to do anything which impairs its
authority.'*

PRESIDENT KWAME NKRUMAH of Ghana,
17 August 1960

THE task of defending the Congo's independence was entrusted
to the UN on 12 July, the day following the entry of Belgian paratroops. Two days before, the Congo had appealed to the UN for
technical assistance. The mutiny had virtually brought all government and public services to a halt. The panic flight of the Belgians
reduced their numbers in Leopoldville from 18,000 to 2,500; in
Luluabourg from 6,000 to 200; in Stanleyville from 5,000 to 300;
in the port of Matadi from 1,800 to 10. Only the gamest and the
lamest Belgians had remained. The flight of the rest wrecked the
plan of resting the Congo's independence on Belgium. There was
nothing to take her place.

The inexperienced Ministers sat with neither staff nor policy at their large idle desks; there were no secretaries or telephone operators. From the start, the Prime Minister had hardly given a moment's thought to the task of governing the country: every moment of his day and most of every night was spent in relentless effort to withstand the blows that came from all sides. On the day of its appeal to the UN the hapless Republic resembled the poet's ship: its sails torn and tattered, seams opening wide; its rudder gone and compass lost.

The UN Secretariat, expecting a summons for technical aid, had already made tentative plans. But these were intended only to complement the Belgians'; they were quite unprepared to take over the administration of the whole country. Still less were they prepared for the appeal that followed immediately on the first: a demand for a UN Force. For the Congo this appeal marked the nadir of its fortunes; for the UN it was an inviting challenge. There was no precedent for what it was asked to do – to rescue a young nation's independence and to nurture it to a freedom it had never known.

The Congo issue came before the Security Council on 13 July. The first hurdle was to get everybody agreed – or at least to avoid the veto. The temptation to bring what was essentially a colonial disaster into 'cold war' politics must have been irresistably strong for the Soviet *bloc*. Yet, on this occasion, the Security Council acted in unison on a question that would normally have divided the West and the communists. The credit for this success belongs to the African group. It was the first time in history that Africa had succeeded in imposing its authority on the Great Powers – an event of some significance. The independent African states (excepting only South Africa) succeeded in doing what no other concert of continental powers had ever achieved – not Europe or Asia, not the Middle East or Latin America. It combined its own forces behind a policy that compelled international agreement. The Western Powers, with a few exceptions, had no motives for wishing to challenge the African states; the Soviet *bloc* did not dare to do so.

MR HAMMARSKJÖLD AND THE AFRICANS

On Tuesday 12 July Hammarskjöld called the African representatives at the UN into consultation over the appeal for technical aid. From the first he recognized the importance of working with and through the African group. After leaving this meeting he heard from Cabot Lodge, the American representative at the UN, that President Eisenhower had been asked by the Congo's Vice-Premier, Antoine Gizenga, to supply military assistance against the Belgians. He had at once rejected this appeal in favour of action within the framework of the UN.* Meanwhile, the Congo's appeal for American intervention had become known in Ghana, where President Nkrumah immediately got to work to persuade Lumumba to appeal to the UN instead.

On that Tuesday evening Hammarskjöld received a cable from President Kasavubu and Prime Minister Lumumba appealing for urgent UN military assistance against a 'Belgian act of aggression'. On Wednesday he received a more urgent cable setting out explicitly the Congo's needs and desires. This cable also included a threat to call in the Bandung Powers if the UN failed to act. Hammarskjöld spent Wednesday morning in consultation with representatives of the Security Council and, especially, with Mongi Slim, the Tunisian member of the Council. As a member of the African group Slim was a key person. The eleven members of the Security Council lunched informally with the Secretary-General where they received their first briefing. A meeting of the Security Council was fixed for eight o'clock the same night.

Hammarskjöld spent the afternoon laying his plans for speedily assembling a UN Force. With his experts he discussed how to stage the operation: setting up communications; obtaining food supplies; and deciding on the pattern for troop recruitment. Kano, Nigeria's air terminal, was fixed as the ideal base; the British Government and Nigeria were at once consulted about its use. Meanwhile, the members of the Security Council were getting instructions from their Governments. The African group met in continuous session throughout the afternoon to brief Slim. The Asian representative on the Security Council, Sir Claude Corea of Ceylon, conferred with the Asian group. Later, Sir Claude and Mongi Slim coordinated the policies of the Afro-Asian group.

---

* The fact that the first appeal went to Washington should not be lost sight of in the subsequent events that led to allegations that Lumumba and his deputy, Gizenga, were in the hands of the Russians.

Hammarskjöld's concern deepened with the afternoon's developments. France and Italy were reported 'difficult' because of their reluctance to appear to side against the Belgians, and because Italy had subjects of its own in the Congo. Britain was threatening to raise objections of a more technical kind. Over all hung the threat of a Russian veto. In the late afternoon Hammarskjöld called in the Soviet delegate, Sobolev, and talked with him for an hour and a half. By this time the African group had drafted an agreed resolution to be submitted by Slim. It was considered and approved by the Asians. Hammarskjöld, too, approved. The African group then set their lobby to work on the Russians. They warned them of the impression the Societ *bloc* would create if they went against African wishes.

THE FIRST SECURITY COUNCIL MEETING

Although the final vote on the African resolution* did not come until 3.22 on the morning of 14 July it had been won before the Security Council went into session.

The representatives of the Belgians and the Congolese faced each other as accuser and defendant before the Security Council. The Congolese spokesman was twenty-eight-year-old Thomas Kanza who, at the time of the Round Table Talks in Brussels, was working as a junior economist with the European Common Market. 'It is not often', he said, 'that barely two weeks after a country has achieved its independence, it is obliged to present itself almost as an accuser before the Security Council because,

---

* 'The Security Council, considering the report of the Secretary-General on a request for United Natic_s action in relation to the Republic of the Congo; Considering the request for military assistance addressed to the Secretary-General by the President and the Prime Minister of the Republic of the Congo; Calls upon the Government of Belgium to withdraw their troops from the territory of the Republic of the Congo; Decides to authorize the Secretary-General to take the necessary steps, in consultation with the Government of the Republic of the Congo, to provide the Government with such military assistance as may be necessary, until, through the efforts of the Congolese Government and with the technical assistance of the United Nations, the national security forces may be able, in the opinion of the Government, to meet fully their tasks; Requests the Secretary-General to report to the Security Council as appropriate.'

contrary to what we might have hoped, the country which was formerly the colonizer, and which normally should have become a friendly country, violated on three occasions the treaty which we signed on 29 June, on the eve of the Congo's accession to independence. The Congolese', he added, 'are prepared to recognize that abuses have been committed.' He outlined four points on which his Government wanted action to be taken – to put an end to the aggressive action of the Belgian troops; the evacuation as soon as possible of those troops; non-recognition of the independence of Katanga; technical assistance.

Belgium's Foreign Minister, Pierre Wigny, spoke in terms both aggrieved and righteous. 'It would have been better ... to have recognized first of all that frightful things have happened, frightful things which, naturally, have caused the departure of the Belgians who trustingly remained among you. Our action', he continued, 'is not aggression. Nor is it an act of madness. It is an action justified not by our hostility towards a people whom we love and to whom we have granted independence, nor by hostility on the part of the Congolese people towards us, but by the fact that the Congolese Government – certain of its members, and perhaps one of them alone* – was incapable of re-establishing order. In these justified, necessary interventions we have always done everything to limit them to the maximum extent possible ... We sent troops. They intervened strictly because of our sacred duty to protect the lives and the honour of our fellow-citizens. The action of our troops was always limited to these specific objectives.' He offered to withdraw Belgian troops as soon as UN troops arrived in sufficient number to guarantee security.

In the debate that followed the Russians were considerably reluctant to submit tamely to acceptance of the Afro-Asian sponsored resolution. They tried skilfully to force openings by going for the obviously popular issues that were not covered by the resolution, and which had been deliberately left out to ensure its quick passage. They proposed an amendment to 'condemn the armed aggression by Belgium'; another called upon Belgium to withdraw its troops 'immediately'; a third proposed that military assistance should be restricted to the African state members of the UN. All these amendments were defeated.

* An obvious reference to M. Patrice Lumumba.

UN STRATEGY

Although the Security Council rose shortly before Thursday's dawn, Hammarskjöld at once took Slim to his office to set the UN operation in motion. His immediate aim was to get troops into the Congo as quickly as possible. While putting the emphasis on African troops, he included two strictly neutralist European countries – Eire and Sweden – to reassure the Belgians. Slim had already obtained permission for Tunisian troops to leave at once. President Nkrumah, too, had offered to dispatch Ghanaian troops as soon as the resolution was passed. Hammarskjöld put through calls to Emperor Haile Selassie, who had thrown himself actively into the spirit of the operation, and to President Tubman of Liberia. Both responded immediately. Britain and Nigeria confirmed their agreement to the use of Kano as a staging post. Another call went through to Dr Ralph Bunche in Leopoldville instructing him to call an immediate conference to reassure the Congolese and the Belgians about the purpose of the UN intervention.

Throughout Thursday Hammarskjöld continued phoning the heads of African states. He also made personal appeals to UN members to send food, supplies, technicians, and aircraft. Within thirty-six hours of the resolution being passed, the Tunisian troops arrived in Leopoldville, just ahead of the Ghanaians. It was the swiftest and largest operation the UN had ever undertaken on its own. Its stock never stood higher.

But the UN enterprise, blessed by a happy start, was rapidly caught up in a web of misunderstandings and suspicions that threatened to bring the entire operation to grief. The Congolese leaders had hoped for two things when they first appealed to the UN: to get the Belgian troops out of the Congo, including Katanga; and to restore the country's integrity by recognizing the illegality of Katanga's declaration of independence. This second point was never clearly spelled out, although it was expressed in the speech Thomas Kanza made to the Security Council.

Hammarskjöld carefully defined his mandate in his explanatory statement to the Security Council, which nobody challenged at the time. He laid it down that the UN Force could not take the initiative in the use of armed force, and could only act in self-defence. It would not take any action making it a party to internal conflicts. By this definition there could be no question of the UN on its own initiative, or with the cooperation of the Central Government, overthrowing the Government of M. Tshombe to restore the Congo's integrity. Nor did the resolution make provision for action in the event of force having to be used to secure the purposes of the resolution. When, therefore, Katanga threatened to resist UN troops by force, Hammarskjöld had no immediate answer to the situation that faced him. He had to return to the Security Council for a fresh mandate. This delay proved almost fatal.

The resolution suffered from one other serious weakness: its insistence on self-defence tied the hands of the UN Force in such a way that it could not intervene to prevent Congolese from killing each other. Had it been otherwise many lives could have been saved. Those who upheld the 'self-defence' restriction imposed on the UN Force rightly insist that this condition is a necessary corollary to non-interference in internal affairs. On the face of it, this argument is incontestable; but its strict application at one time threatened to bring the moral purpose of the Force into contempt. These weaknesses explain many of the difficulties in which Hammarskjöld quickly found himself.

IMPATIENCE AND INTRANSIGENCE

The first crisis of confidence came within a week of the arrival of the UN Force on 15 July. It was produced partly by the understandable but unreasonable impatience of the Congolese leaders over the 'slowness' of the incoming UN troops to take action; and partly by the terms insisted upon by the Belgians for their withdrawal. The target for the Congolese attack was Dr Ralph Bunche.

The weight of the United Nations' vast enterprise had fallen on him. His hotel suite had been transformed into a joint headquarters for the Government of the country and for the Military Command of the UN Forces. Backed by a small staff of UN experts, Dr Bunche was trying to mount two parallel operations:

restaffing the administration, which had virtually ceased to exist, and restoring the technical services to look after health, food supplies, public utilities, and communications. Belgian staff of the University of Lovanium, who had not gone on leave, were recruited to fill the vacant senior positions in the administration; an American economist who happened to be doing research for a thesis was put in charge of the Treasury. Hundreds of technicians supplied by the UN Specialized Agencies were allocated to priority tasks. The effort was herculean. But the task was complicated by the difficulty of getting authorization for policy decisions or actions. The majority of the Ministers were too busily occupied in other ways: government was not their immediate concern; they were preoccupied with the struggle for political survival. The administration was working virtually without a head.

Dr Bunche's other task was to direct the initial operations of the UN Force. He opened negotiations with the Belgians to agree on the 'modalities' for their withdrawal. But Lumumba was in no mood for the niceties of negotiations. On the day after the first handful of troops had arrived, he delivered an ultimatum: either the Belgians were made to withdraw within seventy-two hours, or Soviet troops would be called in. The conservative Senate (representative of five of the six provinces) at once repudiated Lumumba's threat to seek Russian aid. But Lumumba trumped their ace by getting his Cabinet to agree to a resolution agreeing to appeal to the Russians or to any Afro-Asian *bloc* country to send troops unless the UN got the Belgians out of the country.

By 18 July, 4,000 troops from five African countries had arrived in Leopoldville; on the following day Dr Bunche persuaded the Belgians to begin their withdrawal on 20 July, and to complete the operation within three days. But by then the interplay of impatience and delay had produced an untenable position. Lumumba's harassing tactics displeased the African states. Although they shared his impatience, they deplored his threats to call in the Russians.

THE SECOND SECURITY COUNCIL MEETING

The crisis was broken by a second successful intervention by the African group in the Security Council on 21 and 22 July. In collaboration with the Asian states, they sponsored another resolution setting out two objectives. The first was to intensify the pressure on the Belgians to withdraw. The second was to call on all states 'to refrain from any action which might tend to impede the restoration of law and order ... and from any action which might undermine the territorial integrity and the political independence of the Republic of the Congo'. Again they forced agreement on the Security Council.

THE KATANGA LAST DITCH

On 23 July the Belgians completed their withdrawal from the Congo – but not from Katanga. They assembled in large numbers in Tshombe's Republic, and Tshombe was emboldened to defy the UN. His bravado is easily dismissed; the Belgian attitude is less easy to explain. However much they hoped to 'save' Katanga, how did they imagine they could successfully defy the UN? Their intransigence imperilled its efforts to meet the crisis; undermined the temperate policies hitherto pursued by the African states; and soon opened the way for Russian intervention. Whatever might be said in justification of Belgian policies, their prodding Tshombe into defiance of the UN was an act of momentous folly.

The consequences soon followed: first Guinea and then Ghana threatened that, if the UN did not get the Belgians out of Katanga, they would feel free to place their forces under the direct command of the Congo Government to accomplish this purpose. This action is sometimes cited as evidence of the lack of the sincerity by Africans in supporting the UN. The record shows that both Ghana and Guinea said they would act only if the UN failed to implement the Security Council resolutions. Once the Security Council reaffirmed its decisions, both President Sékou Toure and President Nkrumah at once expressed their complete confidence in Hammarskjöld. But between 23 July – the day of the evacuation of the Belgians from the five provinces of the Congo – and 12 August, when the UN Force was finally allowed to enter Katanga, the internal situation had deteriorated to a point almost past recovery. The strain between Lumumba and Hammarskjöld was near breaking-point.

During those critical weeks too, the Soviet *bloc* was able to exploit the troubled situation to such an extent that Lumumba felt he could rely on them as an alternative to the UN to achieve his purpose – expelling the last of the Belgians and bringing Katanga back under the authority of the Central Government. The Russians felt sufficiently confident to start a campaign against Hammarskjöld and the policies of the UN Command. They 'condemned the imperialist aggression against the Republic of the Congo' and declared they would not hesitate 'to take resolute measures to rebuff the aggressors'. They also announced they were sending food, medical teams and equipment, and 100 trucks with instructors to the Congo; already their aircraft were engaged in the airlift of UN troops; but, unlike all the other countries, their gifts were not channelled through the UN.

The language of the Russians gladdened Lumumba's heart, as indeed it might. Here was one power which was ready to deal with the Belgians. His attitude gravely disquieted the African group, with the exception of Guinea. They feared the 'cold war' was coming perilously close to Africa, and accordingly intensified their pressure on Hammarskjöld to enter Katanga.

On 4 August, twenty-two days after the first UN decision – Dr Bunche went to Katanga to inform Tshombe that the UN Force would enter his Province. Two days later he returned to report on 'the unqualified and unyielding opposition of Mr Tshombe'. To the Congolese leaders it looked like betrayal. Was this the powerful world force they had heard so much about, a power that flinched before the threats of the contemptuous Tshombe?

Seen in these realistic Congolese terms the questions were fair. But Hammarskjöld was troubled by different considerations. 'The introduction of army units into Katanga by the UN would be possible only by resort to the use of armed force on its part', he said on hearing Dr Bunche's report. 'Such an initiative by the UN Force is against the principles established by the Security Council for the operation of the Force, and against the conditions on which various contributing countries have agreed to send units into the Force.' Once again he went back to the Security Council. Hammarskjöld's defence of his position was that he did not believe that 'we help the Congolese people by actions in which Africans kill Africans, or Congolese kill Congolese, and that will remain my guiding principle for the future'. Lumumba was not to be swayed by such arguments.

THE THIRD SECURITY COUNCIL MEETING

When the Secretary-General faced the Security Council for the third time on 8 August, he did not try to argue against the use of force if necessary to get into Katanga. He warned that the threat of armed opposition could no longer justify further delays in putting UN troops into Katanga. Immediate action was needed to effect the withdrawal of Belgian troops whose presence was 'the main cause of continued danger'. By then he was thoroughly alarmed. 'The problem facing the Congo', he said, 'is one of peace or war – and not only in the Congo.'

The position inside the Security Council was becoming more difficult with each meeting. The Russians were becoming surer of their ground, and less amenable to African arguments. They proposed to compel the Secretary-General to 'use any means' to get the Belgians out of Katanga. Inside the African group, too, it had become more difficult to work for conciliation, especially since Lumumba also was no longer so ready to listen to their advice. Despite these difficulties, for the third time since the beginning of the Congo crisis, the African group and the Asians succeeded in presenting another agreed resolution to the Security Council. Although the Russians threatened to stick to their own resolution, they finally gave way. The Security Council warned the Belgian Government to withdraw its troops from Katanga immediately; they declared the entry of the UN Force into Katanga to be necessary for the fulfilment of their resolutions; and they reaffirmed their policy that the UN Force 'would not be a party to, or in any way intervene in, or be used to influence, the outcome of any internal conflict, constitutional or otherwise'.

Lumumba accepted this decision; amity was again restored between him and Hammarskjöld. This truce was to be the last. A fresh crisis came within a few days over the interpretation of the last part of this resolution.

UN IN KATANGA

Hammarskjöld entered Katanga on 12 August with the UN Force, after Belgium had recognized the limit of world patience. Tshombe blandly pretended he had never objected to the UN presence as such. What he objected to was that the UN operation should become a spearhead for action by the Central Government. This was a critical question. If the UN went in without representatives of the Lumumba government, their authority over Katanga would still be zero. Lumumba saw this danger, but Hammarskjöld refused to allow him or anybody else from the Central Government to accompany the UN Force into Katanga.

Was this a wise decision? Even now the question is not merely hypothetical. It goes to the roots of UN policy in the Congo. By the decision of the third meeting of the Security Council, the UN clearly recognized the integrity of the Congo. But it made no proposals for re-establishing this integrity. In fact, it ruled out any initiative on its own part. The UN's own purpose in entering Katanga was to remove the Belgian troops, not to remove Tshombe. How to deal with him was a matter left to the Congolese to decide. Thus the UN action did no more than clear the way for mediation.

Hammarskjöld was quite clear on the interpretation of the Security Council's decision. The UN Force could not be used on behalf of the Central Government to subdue or to force the Katanga provincial government to a specific line of action. United Nations facilities could not be used to transport Central Government civilian or military representatives against the decision of the Katanga provincial government. The UN Force had neither the duty nor the right to protect Central Government representatives arriving in Katanga, beyond what followed from its general duty to maintain law and order. On the other hand, the United Nations had no right to forbid the Central Government to take any action which by its own means, in accordance with the Purposes and Principles of the Charter, it could carry through in relation to Katanga.

Lumumba rejected this 'unilateral and erroneous' interpretation. In a heated, quick-fire exchange of letters on 14 and 15 August the Prime Minister made it clear that the UN could not be allowed to act as a neutral organization in the Congo. He insisted that the UN Force should 'be used to subdue the rebel government in Katanga'. All non-African troops, he demanded, should be immediately withdrawn from Katanga. (The Swedes had been used initially for this operation; later Mali troops were put in as well.) The correspondence was rounded off with Lumumba accusing Hammarskjöld of losing the confidence of the Congolese, and of being a puppet of the colonialists. Hammarskjöld acidly challenged Lumumba to take his case to the Security Council. So back they went to the Security Council for the fourth time. Before the Council met, *cadres* of Congolese troops attacked UN personnel, alleging that Belgian spies were working among them. Leopoldville was threatened again with chaos.

These repeated crises began to have their effect within the African group. Guinea moved towards a militant, unilateral position. The Tunisians were inclined to move in the opposite direction, losing confidence in the Prime Minister. Dr Nkrumah, too, was anxious about the trend of Lumumba's policy. On 19 August he took the unusual step of sending a delegation to Lumumba, preceded by an urgent cable. 'Neither you personally nor the people of the Congo have anything to gain by the complete breakdown of law and order', he cabled. 'I beg you to exercise a restraining influence upon the activities of the Force Publique and police.' And in a personal letter he wrote: 'I am quite certain that the Secretary-General of the United Nations will never allow Belgians to re-establish themselves anywhere in the Congo. If the situation continues to be chaotic as it is in Leopoldville at the moment, there is a grave danger of our dear Congo becoming a battleground between East and West. This last will be a disaster for us in Africa.'

THE FOURTH SECURITY COUNCIL MEETING

The fourth meeting of the Security Council (21–22 August) was the toughest of all. Hammarskjöld's personal reputation was now at stake. But, as on the three previous occasions, he had the solid support of the African group. Although no longer uncritical, they were still unshaken in their determination to work within the framework of the UN. No resolution was passed by the fourth meeting of the Security Council, but Mr Hammarskjöld withstood a scorching attack from the Soviet and Polish delegates to win what amounted to a vote of confidence. His interpretation of the Council's resolutions was upheld; and his proposal to set up an Advisory Council of representatives of all the countries which had sent troops to the Congo was approved. Faced with this decision Lumumba climbed down. Once more he said he was 'satisfied'.

THE FIFTH SECURITY COUNCIL MEETING

But this 'satisfaction', too, was short-lived. Towards the end of August a new pattern of events began to unfold in the Congo; these will be considered presently. Their impact on the UN was to make it almost impossible to pursue policies of non-intervention, while at the same time trying to maintain security and to keep the administration working. The African group had its loyalties strained to the limit, both within its own organization and in its relations with Lumumba and Hammarskjöld. The explosion came at the fifth meeting of the Security Council, which lasted for two days, from 15 to 17 September. Hammarskjöld went into this meeting not only with his personal reputation at stake, but with the authority of the UN itself called into question. For the first time since the beginning of the crisis the African group failed to impose its will on the Security Council. The Russians, finally, decided to risk going against the African States. They challenged the UN handling of the Congo issue by calling for the removal of the UN Command. They obviously gambled on winning Lumumba's wholehearted support, and were strongly encouraged to believe that they could shake the unity of the Afro-Asian group, but they were immediately proved wrong. The Afro-Asians unanimously supported the proposals made by Hammarskjöld in his report to the Security Council. These requested all states to refrain from any action which might tend to impede the restoration of law and order; called on all Congolese to seek a speedy solution of their internal conflicts by peaceful means; insisted that no military assistance should be given to the Congo except through the UN; and called upon all states, without prejudice to the sovereign rights of the Congo, to refrain from sending materials of war and military personnel, directly or indirectly, to the Congo, except through the channels of the UN.

When the Security Council adopted these proposals – with their implicit criticisms of the Russians as well as of the Belgians – the Russians used their veto. An emergency session of the General Assembly was immediately arranged under the 'uniting for peace' resolution. Confronted by all the members of the UN, the Russians maintained their frontal assault. Their special target was still the Secretary-General. He was accused of committing 'treason to the interests of the Congolese people'; and criticized for not showing 'even the minimum of objectivity', and for acting as a 'screen for the colonialists'. The Russian challenge was turned into a *débâcle*; their veto was overridden with not a single country outside the Soviet *bloc* supporting them. The Afro-Asian resolution, as quoted above, was adopted by seventy votes to none, with eleven abstentions. These included the Soviet *bloc*, France, and South Africa.

Chapter 13

PROMISE AND FAILURE

'Patrice Lumumba, you are the man we need; you are hope and the hope of our future. . . . Martyr of freedom, child of our fatherland, symbol of freedom, protector of our ancestors' rights, valiant soldier, let your agonizing enemies watch your triumph and our glory.'

Editorial in Congo *Independance*

THE high hopes with which the UN went into the Congo were not immediately justified by events. By the end of September it had lost its initiative. The Government it had come to assist was in ruins. Its technical services were throttled because of the need for an effective authority through whom they could work. The policy of the UN Command was under heavy attack, and the Secretary-General had himself become the centre of 'cold war' politics, largely because of his role in the Congo. It was a dismal anti-climax.

The events leading up to the complete breakdown of government in the Congo can be conveniently traced from 15 August, just one month after the first UN troops arrived in response to the appeal from the Central Government. By then the UN Force had virtually secured its primary objective: the Belgian troops had left, and a UN contingent had been allowed to enter Katanga. The explicit instructions given to Hammarskjöld by the Security Council had been fulfilled; the other duties imposed on him – to provide technical assistance, and to help maintain security without interfering in the Congo's domestic affairs – could be achieved only through cooperation with Lumumba's Government.

Lumumba was left with two main objectives after the Belgians' expulsion: to secure effective power within his shaky coalition Government, and to restore Katanga to the authority of the Central Government. He sought UN support for these two aims, but Hammarskjöld refused. Not only did he refuse to allow the UN Force to be used against Katanga, but he made it virtually impossible for the Congo Government to take direct action by itself. Not altogether unreasonably, from his point of view, Lumumba saw the UN presence as a guarantee for the continued separate existence of Katanga, unless the deadlock could be broken by some different method. He refused, however, to consider negotiating with Tshombe because such negotiations could only proceed on the basis of a federal solution, which touched the central problem of Congolese politics. To concede on this point would have weakened Lumumba's position, and strengthened the federalists'. He refused to abdicate. Instead, he rounded on the UN and began to pursue two contradictory policies. While publicly threatening to call in the aid of 'another Power', he privately took up the Russian offer of aid made on 31 July. But he did not tell either the President, Joseph Kasavubu, or his Foreign Secretary, Justin Bomboka. At the same time he asked for the active support of the African States against the UN decisions (as interpreted by Hammarskjöld), and for a military campaign against Katanga. The Russians responded; the African States did not.

On the diplomatic front the Russians backed Lumumba's attack on Hammarskjöld's decision not to accept orders from his Government. This issue came to a head at the Security Council meeting on 23 August, when the African States supported Hammarskjöld's interpretation, and compelled the Russians to withdraw their censure motion on the Secretary-General. Lumumba, too, declared himself satisfied with the outcome. Yet three days later he was back in the fray with a demand that the UN Force should be withdrawn. This policy was unanimously repudiated by the Congolese Senate. Lumumba next took his case to the 'Little Summit' of thirteen African States which met in Leopoldville on 25 August; again he met with failure. Let down by both the African States and the UN, Lumumba decided to 'go it alone' with the help of the Russians.

Soviet aid, unlike others, went directly to the Government, instead of being channelled through the UN. The Russians delivered 100 military trucks and 29 Ilyushin transport planes, together with 200 technicians. This transport enabled Lumumba to send hand-picked units of the Force Publique to subdue the dissident 'Diamond State' proclaimed by Albert Kalonji in Kasai. More than 1,000 Baluba tribesmen were killed.

THINGS FALL APART

That was the situation on 5 September, the day on which everything began to fall apart. On that day, Lumumba's uneasy coalition finally broke up. The President dismissed him as Prime Minister, and appointed Joseph Ileo in his place. The coalition had always been a shaky affair. The federalists, though displeased with the Prime Minister's erratic policies, had closed their eyes to his actions, hoping that he would expend himself in the effort to impose his personal authority. They had hesitated to act sooner, knowing they could not command sufficient support to make their power effective. But though they were not yet ready to act when they did, events drove them to do so before Russian aid could tip the internal balance of power in Lumumba's favour, and because they felt they could no longer ignore the mounting chaos and the drift to civil war.

The UN representatives in the Congo were equally alarmed. Lumumba's unwillingness to cooperate, his secret negotiations with the Russians, and his determination to secure his ends by the use of force, made a mockery of the UN Force, which was supposed to maintain security. They felt a desperate need for any legal authority with which they could cooperate to carry out the desires of the Security Council. When Kasavubu acted against Lumumba, the UN at once recognized the legality of his action, without even waiting to see whether he could establish his authority. In the event he could not. The Senate refused to confirm the President's dismissal of the Prime Minister, and the Prime Minister's dismissal of the President. Although both leaders were re-established in office by the Senate, the *status quo* had in fact been destroyed. There were now two rival Governments, Lumumba's and Ileo's, each appealing to the people and to the troops for support. It was a situation ripe for civil war.

Faced with this threat the UN representatives in Leopoldville acted under their mandate to maintain security. They feared two immediate dangers: that the use of Leopoldville radio by either or both sides would whip up national feeling to the point of open conflict; and that rival commanders of the Force Publique would bring their troops into the capital. Without waiting to consult Hammarskjöld, the UN organization in the Congo ordered the closing of the radio station and of all airports. When Lumumba attempted to force his way into the radio station, his entry was barred by Ghanaian troops acting under UN orders. The popular Press in Britain gave the impression that this action was taken under the orders of one of Ghana's British officers; the action was in fact taken by a Ghanaian Sergeant. Two British lieutenants serving with the Ghana Army came on the scene only after Lumumba had been stopped. The Ileo Government found a way round the ban. Exploiting the good relations between Kasavubu and Foulbert Youlou, the President of the (former French) Congo Republic across the river, they obtained access to Radio Congo in Brazzaville. Thus only the voice of Kasavubu was heard. After a few days the ban was dropped.

A new factor now entered the picture. Colonel Mobutu, a twenty-eight-year-old army officer (formerly a political journalist and a trained accountant), used his command over the companies of the Force Publique then in the capital to proclaim army rule. While acknowledging the authority of President Kasavubu as Head of State, he ordered the dismissal of both Lumumba's and Ileo's Governments. He shut down the parliament, formed a Government of University Students, and ordered the immediate withdrawal of the Soviet *bloc* representatives. He followed this by threatening to demand the withdrawal of Guinean and Ghanaian troops on the grounds that they were interfering in internal politics.

While Ileo accepted Colonel Mobutu's orders, Lumumba did not. For several weeks the capital witnessed a bewildering change of fortunes. Lumumba and his lieutenants were only just saved from death; later they were arrested, and escaped. Members of Mobutu's 'Government' had similar experiences. Lumumba sought the protection of Ghanaian troops; members of his personal staff fled to sympathetic embassies. Claims and counter-claims of rightful authority came from all sides. But in all this chaos and tension not a single person was killed; nor was a single politician held in effective confinement.

Foreign Press representatives were inclined to view these events as tragi-comedy. But a more accurate perspective would be to see them as a contest between rivals carrying on a vigorous dialogue in public, with each side striking postures and making grandiose claims in attempts to out-manoeuvre the other. Though it perhaps looks ridiculous to outsiders, there is something to be said for a typically African cultural pattern which enables bitter rivalries to exist without either party actually harming the other physically.

The explanation of what happened was that no side felt itself strong enough to take an irrevocable step. Power belonged nowhere, and the UN was helpless to act. The African States tried to reconcile the rivals, but their efforts were continually frustrated. This was the situation in the Congo when the Security Council met on the eve of the 1960 UN General Assembly, where the Congo was tossed into the arena of the cold war. The Soviet Government charged the UN with acting in the Congo on behalf of 'a coalition of colonialists'. The African and Asian leaders criticized some of Hammarskjöld's policies, but with restraint and understanding.

Quite rightly, the Soviet Government had insisted* that the events in the Congo should be seen as 'a serious test of the impartiality of the United Nations apparatus'. Did the U N, in fact, behave inpartially? To what extent did its policies contribute to the collapse of the Central Government? Could different policies have avoided this collapse? These questions are as important for the future as for an understanding of what went wrong. But before trying to answer them it is necessary to consider the role played by external forces in the Congo.

* Statement by the Soviet Government, 1 September 1960.

Chapter 14

ROLE OF THE AFRICAN STATES

'Once we admit our impotence to solve the question of the Congo primarily with our own African resources, we tacitly admit that real self-government on the African continent is impossible.... I would not be so presumptuous as to put forward a Monroe doctrine for Africa. I must say, however, that the Great Powers of the world should realize that very often African questions can be settled by African states if there is no outside intervention or interference.'

PRESIDENT KWAME NKRUMAH, 8 August 1960

PAN-AFRICANISM met its first real challenge in the Congo: previously, the emotional urge towards continental unity had been tested only in committee rooms and on conference platforms. Disagreements privately arrived at could be publicly hidden behind resounding resolutions denouncing colonialism, racialism, and imperialism; and by pledges of undivided loyalty to the concepts of an undefined African personality. Pan-Africanism thrived on its search for unity; in the Congo it faced the need for agreed decision speedily taken in response to sharply changing situations.

I am not concerned here with a discussion of the nature and forces of Pan-Africanism, except in so far as it helps to clarify the role of the African States in the Congo. The manner in which this group behaved, and the tensions that exist within it, will undoubtedly have important repercussions; to pursue these now would be irrelevant to the central theme of this book.

The previous chapter described the unanimity maintained by the members of the Conference of Independent African States*

* Cameroons, Congo, Ethiopia, Ghana, Guinea, Libya, Liberia, Morocco, Nigeria, Sudan, Somalia, Tunisia, U.A.R. The Algerian Provisional Government is also recognized as a full member. The bulk of the French Community states and Nigeria became UN members only in October, and were therefore not active participants in the African group during the period under consideration.

represented in the African group at the UN. The two non-participant members were the Cameroons Republic – the only member of the French Community which formally adheres to the Conference – and Somalia; neither sent troops to the Congo.

The African group work largely through informal machinery. Their permanent nucleus are the African Representatives at the United Nations. This nucleus was paralleled in the Congo by the African Ambassadors, who frequently consulted each other.

THE ROLE OF GHANA

The initiative in the Congo lay in Accra, where President Nkrumah kept in daily contact with Leopoldville and the UN Headquarters, and carried on rapid consultations with other African states through his Ambassadors in their capitals, as well as through their Ambassadors in Accra.

Dr Nkrumah's leadership role is due to two factors. A close personal relationship exists between him and Patrice Lumumba. Before independence, the two leaders had tentatively explored the possibility of the Congo formally adhering to the Ghana–Guinea Union*. Although no definite decision had been taken, their identity of views and of possible interests explains the special role Ghana played in the Congo. The second factor is Dr Nkrumah's essentially revolutionary view of Pan-Africanism. For him it is not just a cosy notion of a lot of African leaders trying to work together. He has staked his reputation, and Ghana's, on a militant campaign to build a United States of Africa. Critics accuse him of 'empire building'; a more useful concept would be to see him as the champion of an idea which transcends countries and personalities. Although he has created organizations of his own design to foster his policies, he has always been careful to work within the framework of the Conference of Independent African States,

* This Union exists in name only, although tentative steps have been taken to allow for continuous interchange of views between the two states by each, theoretically, admitting a Minister from the other to its Cabinet. Relations between these two countries in no sense conform to the general idea of what a Union should involve. The increasingly independent role played by Guinea in the Congo (though not in the African group at the U N) suggests growing differences within the Union.

and within the less rigidly structured All-African People's Organization. On a wider front he has worked within the framework of the Commonwealth of Nations, and on the international front he has worked within the framework of the United Nations. But within the limitations imposed by these wider organizations he has consistently tried to maintain the initiative for his idea of a political union of African States. It is this concept of a 'political union' that divides Pan-Africanists. In the Congo Dr Nkrumah was well-placed to promote an extension of his idea of 'political union' between African States. He was never afraid of committing his own Government.

The threatening dangers in the Congo had been raised by the African States for the first time at their second conference in Addis Ababa in May 1960. Their concern was about continued Belgian interference in the internal affairs of the. Congo, and especially about the apparent inability of the Congolese leaders to come to an agreement in forming their first National Government. This concern was reflected in a proposal by the Nigerian delegation for a 'good offices' committee to be sent to the Congo, an idea vigorously criticized on the grounds that it encouraged support for the view that Congolese leaders were incapable of managing their own affairs. Nevertheless, African leaders did, in fact, later play an important part in persuading Lumumba to accept Kasavubu as the first Head of State. Ghana's intervention with Lumumba was especially influential – a fact privately acknowledged at the time by Kasavubu.

Ghana's support for a national government including both the Pan-Africanists (Lumumba's supporters) and the federalists ('tribal nationalists') went against the grain. Dr Nkrumah is uncompromisingly committed to a strong, centralized form of government – 'centralized democracy'. He regards federalists as the harbingers of Africa's balkanization. 'In my view,' he has said, 'any person who talks of a federal type of constitution for the Congo is a supporter of the imperialist cause.'* Nevertheless, his realistic assessment of the situation in Leopoldville on the eve of independence was that Belgian influence could only be effectively removed, and Congolese unity established, through a Government that rested on both Lumumba and Kasavubu. This expedient

* Address to Ghana National Assembly, 8 August 1960.

has remained the guiding principle of nearly all the African States.

The intervention of African States on the side of the Congolese was officially proposed for the first time by Dr Nkrumah at a Press Conference in Accra on 6 August. He declared that the behaviour of the Belgian Government over Katanga created a situation which, if not firmly and immediately dealt with, would constitute a major threat to world peace. If no UN solution was forthcoming, Ghana would be willing to fight alone, if necessary, with the Congo 'against Belgian troops and other forces maintained and supplied from Belgium.' But he added, 'my Government believes that if such a struggle did arise, Ghana and other African States would not be without aid and assistance from other countries which value, as a principle, the conception of African independence.'

Dr Nkrumah followed up this initiative by a dispatch to the heads of other African States proposing joint action through the UN. 'A special responsibility, in my opinion, rests upon all African States to take vigorous steps to reassert the authority of the United Nations. I consider it is essential for all African States to act with complete solidarity and to support a common policy. ... Such unity is also essential to prevent outside interference in the affairs of the African continent.' He added that he believed the UN would act against the Belgians, but 'if the worst came to the worst and no United Nations solution was found and therefor ,Ghana had to give military assistance to the Congo outside the framework of the United Nations, Ghana would have your sympathy in taking this action. I hope we shall also have your support in any military steps which become necessary through the failure of the United Nations to deal with this issue.'

The response to Dr Nkrumah's appeal was unanimously favourable, although several of the African States felt that his declaration of intention to 'go it alone' with the Congo was somewhat flamboyant and cast a reflection on his colleagues. But this was a passing irritation. Accra's determination to show that among equals it is the most militant has become a recognized feature of the African scene. But on the question of the Congo, Ghana found that she was by no means the most militant. Guinea began to outflank her on the left.

RELATIONS WITH MR LUMUMBA

Although the African States were willing to give full backing to Lumumba's Government, the Prime Minister's erratic policies imposed an increasing strain on their loyalty as August lengthened into September. It was not only that he was difficult to deal with; his personal quarrels with Dr Ralph Bunche and Mr Hammarskjöld, his nagging doubts about the UN and especially his connivance at attacks on UN personnel by members of the Force Publique, and his private negotiations with the Russians, all contributed to dissension and division. At the UN the African group formulated their policies after consultation with Lumumba; but they were not guided by him. None of the African leaders was willing, for obvious reasons, to criticize him publicly. They were conscious of the need for African States not to interfere in the internal affairs of another independent state, however great the temptation to do so. Dr Nkrumah came nearer than most to criticizing Lumumba openly. After the attack on UN personnel at Leopoldville airport in the middle of August, Dr Nkrumah sent a delegation to warn Lumumba of the dangers of his policy.*

The situation by the middle of August was extremely critical. With the future of the UN operation in the Congo at stake, the African group worked hard to prevent this disaster. Although at times Guinea seemed less in accord with this policy than the rest of the African States, Dr Nkrumah vigorously championed the UN's cause. He summoned a special meeting of his National Assembly to 'reaffirm our faith in the purpose and principles of the United Nations and its Charter.... In the United Nations lies the only hope for the future of all nations.'

The African group was under considerable pressure from Lumumba to provide him with troops to enable him to invade and overthrow Tshombe's Government in Katanga. Although Guinea, Ghana, and the UAR publicly affirmed their willingness to consider doing so all three made their offer conditional on the UN's refusal to take steps to restore the integrity of the Congo. None of the African States was willing to settle the Katanga question outside the framework of the UN, or at least not until an effort

* See page 137.

had been made to reach agreement through conciliation. Tshombe himself appealed to Dr Nkrumah to come to Katanga with a view to discussing some settlement, and Nkrumah was willing to do so. But Lumumba withheld his consent. His view was that no settlement was possible with Tshombe except on the latter's terms. He repeatedly insisted that the ultimate constitution of the Congo could be settled only in the manner agreed: that Parliament should act as a Constituent Assembly to decide the country's future.

Dr Nkrumah's own position was unequivocal. 'The proposal to establish a loose federation in the Congo is merely an attempt by those who failed to detach Katanga from the Congo Republic to get balkanization of the Congo by the backdoor', he said. Nevertheless, he went on, 'the question of a constitution for the Congo is entirely a matter for the Congolese people themselves to decide'.*

Although Lumumba appears at no time to have lost his confidence in Dr Nkrumah – they constantly exchanged personal letters on most intimate terms – his staff in Leopoldville began to reflect the influences that were gaining weight in his own mind. The Guineans were prominently in attendance; other members of his entourage were drawn from supporters of the 'Conakry line' with its anti-Western, though not necessarily pro-Soviet, bias. In this situation the non-revolutionary wing of the Pan-Africanists (especially Tunisia and Liberia) found themselves increasingly isolated. The Sudan was inclined to take a back-seat, while Ethiopia and Morocco leaned towards the position of the Ghanaians and the UAR. The latter state played only a minor role in the Congo, although its voice was naturally influential in the African group.

Relations between Lumumba and the African group were finally brought to a head by the 'Little Summit' of African States† held in Leopoldville from 25 to 31 August. Lumumba's hopes from this conference were that he would get backing for his view that the UN was too greatly guided by 'colonialist influences', and support for military action against Katanga. He was particularly hostile to the Tunisians, whose UN representative, Mongi Slim,

* Address to the Ghana National Assembly, 8 August 1960.
† Algeria, Congo, Ethiopia, Ghana, Guinea, Libya, Liberia, Morocco, Sudan, Togoland, Tanganyika, Tunisia, United Arab Republic.

was singled out for a cold attack in the officially-sponsored *Congo* on the eve of the conference. Its discussions, though at times heated, ended in agreement, with only the Guineans inclining to a minority position. Having heard Lumumba, the conference decided against his views on all except one issue. They praised the work of the UN and regretted the 'incidents' which had interfered with what they felt should have been the whole-hearted co-operation between the UN and the Congo Government. They unanimously agreed to send a message of appreciation to Dr Ralph Bunche*, who had been fiercely criticized by the Congo Prime Minister. They emphasized the importance of 'harmonizing' all aid to the Congo within the programme of the UN. Their only division of opinion was over action against Katanga. While condemning the 'secession and colonialist manoeuvres' and pledging support to the integrity of the Congo, the conference offered nothing positive in reply to Lumumba's appeal for direct action to overthrow Tshombe's Government. In private sessions efforts had been made to persuade Lumumba to begin negotiations with Tshombe; but no agreement came. Despite this growing gulf between Lumumba and the African States, great care was taken not to estrange the Congo Prime Minister – although the Tunisians were notably out of patience with him, and he with them.

NATIONALISTS' CORRESPONDENCE

The African States were never willing to see Lumumba sacrificed, especially not to the forces of Kasavubu. Tunisia, and perhaps Liberia, were less staunch in this attitude than most others. The relationship between Lumumba and Nkrumah, however, remained intimate, as is shown by the letters which Colonel Mobutu decided to publish in an attempt to prove that Ghana's President was 'plotting' in the Congo. For the sake of clarity it is necessary to keep two points separate: the role of Ghana's troops in the Congo, whose loyalty to the UN Command has never been questioned except by Colonel Mobutu; and the advice proferred to Lumumba by Dr Nkrumah.

* Soviet propaganda represented this distinguished Negro leader as 'an American imperialist'.

His letters, though revealing, contain nothing surprising. His advice to Lumumba proceeds along precisely the same lines that he had followed in establishing his own power in Ghana. His tactics rested on the basis of isolating and dealing with opponents singly; not striking before he was quite sure of success; mobilizing all possible support to increase his strength; not offending those who might be useful; and trusting none except tested friends.

The propriety of Dr Nkrumah's giving advice to the Congo Prime Minister cannot be questioned. This is the normal business of allies. All that might be questioned would be any indication in the correspondence that Ghana was proposing, through its troops or in any other way, to interfere actively in the Congo. No such evidence appears. On the contrary, Dr Nkrumah's counsel is for caution and restraint. He explains but does not criticize the action of Ghanaian troops acting against Lumumba in carrying out UN orders; and he continues to plead for cooperation with the UN. His advice on tactics is not relevant to charges of interference.

Dr Nkrumah had never made any secret of his distrust of federalist leaders like Kasavubu and Tshombe; at the same time, as his letters show, he recognized the need to maintain national unity, and to avoid precipitate action at a time when the Congo was in chaos. One final point must be borne in mind in trying to understand Nkrumah's letters: he is writing to a bitterly frustrated leader, a man increasingly difficult to influence. He is clearly trying to get in on Lumumba's 'wavelength'.

In response to a letter from Lumumba referring to the 'treachery of Kasavubu', Dr Nkrumah wrote on 12 September: 'You cannot afford, my brother, to be harsh and uncompromising. Do not force Kasavubu out now. It will bring you too much trouble in Leopoldville when you want calm there now. Do not make an issue of [Kasavubu's] treachery now, or even of Tshombe's treachery. Time will come to deal with them. Let sleeping dogs lie.' He urges Lumumba to work 'even with the bitterest political enemies' until his position is consolidated, and he warns him: 'You must not push the United Nations out until you have consolidated your position.' Looking more deeply beneath the surface, he calls attention to the danger that the people would not continue to go hungry while the politicians quarrelled.

This letter gives some sound advice on Cabinet reorganization, working through a small Inner Cabinet for quick decisions (Nkrumah's own method of working), and appointing a separate technical Cabinet to ensure effective cooperation with the UN and with foreign states.

'You may be sure', Nkrumah confided to Lumumba, 'that in any crisis I will mobilize the Afro-Asian *bloc* and other friendly nations as in the present attempt to dethrone you. Whenever in doubt consult me. Brother, we have been in the game for some time now and we know how to handle the imperialists and the colonialists. The only colonialist or imperialist I trust is a dead one. If you do not want to bring the Congo into ruin, follow the advice I have given.' And he ends up by saying that if Lumumba failed he would have only himself to blame; but failure would be a great blow to the African liberation movement.

BASIS OF POLICY

Up to this point it is easy to define the main lines of policy pursued by the African States. They took their stand behind the Congo Central Government (with Kasavubu as President and Lumumba as Prime Minister), and against the Katanga secessionists. They vigorously defended the status and authority of the UN in the Congo. They opposed all efforts to extend the cold war into Africa. They sought to avert the settlement of internal problems by the use of military force, counselling reconciliation and peaceful negotiations. While giving freely of their advice to the Congolese all, except Guinea, were careful to avoid direct intervention in the Congo's internal affairs. At the same time they kept themselves free to develop and expound their own policies at the UN.

This outline of policy was broadly supported by the African group. There were, of course, differences in the interpretation of some of the principles, and these gradually led to a weakening in the purposefulness that had been such a feature of the African group's earlier interventions in the UN. Nevertheless, so long as the Central Government remained intact it was possible for the African States to avoid becoming actively involved in the rivalry between the federalists and the unitarians. But after Kasavubu's initiative in dismissing his Prime Minister, it was more difficult to avoid taking sides.

Guinea was uncompromisingly in favour of hoisting Lumumba back into power, with or without Kasavubu. Tunisia took the opposite line; they were ready to write Lumumba off as a hopeless proposition. Ghana, Morocco, the UAR, and Ethiopia formed themselves into a 'good offices' committee to work for reconciliation between Kasavubu and Lumumba, holding firmly to the original policy that the UN could recognize only the 'legitimacy' of the Government which had invited its intervention. The arguments for such a policy were straightforward.

To recognize either Kasavubu or Lumumba separately would be to recognize a Government that did not have the backing of the people. The will of the people, as expressed by the National Assembly before it had been prorogued, was to divide its power between the two leaders. Colonel Mobutu was a young interloper with only the support of a remnant of the Force Publique, trying to impose his views on the country, and with no kind of mandate from the people. To acknowledge any Government that did not rest on some recognizable basis of legitimacy would involve the creation of a dangerous precedent in Africa. If the African States lent their support to such a precedent, it could open the way in the future for 'colonialists' to help overthrow other legitimate governments and to replace them with 'stooge governments' who could then appeal to the UN for recognition and support. The only safe course was to proceed from a recognition of where the people's mandate lay.

ATTITUDE TO THE UN

It was on this issue of legitimacy that the most serious difference of opinion developed within the African group, and between it and Hammarskjöld. He recognized Kasavubu's action as constitutionally justified under the Fundamental Laws which give the President the right to dismiss the Prime Minister, provided his action is countersigned by constitutionally responsible Ministers. The Prime Minister, though, is not entitled under any circumstances to dismiss the Head of State.

By recognizing the Ileo Government, the UN put itself against Lumumba. Had the Ileo Government survived, the situation might have been put beyond legal argument; but it did not. The

Senate's action in confirming both Kasavubu and Lumumba in their old positions created a new situation – one for which the UN could find no immediate answer. It was, therefore, left with no authority on which to rely, until Colonel Mobutu set himself up as the government. The UN, in desperation, dealt with Mobutu and his team; but it had virtually no African support for this decision. Although the majority of the African States were strongly critical of Hammarskjöld on this question, they determinedly refused to criticize him publicly and continued to support his general policies in the Security Council and in the Assembly. They acted in this way for two reasons. They did not want to open a breach between themselves and the Secretary-General which would allow the Great Powers to get at each other's throats; and they patiently hoped and worked for a solution that would offer a legal alternative to Mobutu.

The majority of the African States were also disturbed by the actions of the UN representatives in the Congo in closing the radio station and the airport. Their feeling was that this action, whether intentionally or not, helped Kasavubu. Why, they asked, did the UN not at least try to stop Radio Congo* from broadcasting Kasavubu's statements if it was genuinely intended to keep both contestants off the air?

But although most of the members of the African group believed that 'foreign interests' – that is, Belgian and French – were behind Kasavubu's attempt to overthrow Lumumba, they did not suggest for a moment that the UN representatives in the Congo had anything to do with it. Nor, once the Senate reconfirmed the President in office, did they raise any objections to accepting his position.

* When France conceded independence to the French Congo she secured a lien for thirty years on the powerful Radio Brazzaville for her own programmes. The Congo government in Brazzaville established a separate Radio Congo which uses the buildings and facilities of Radio Brazzaville. The broadcasts by Kasavubu were made from Radio Congo and not Radio Brazzaville.

Chapter 15

POWER POLITICS IN THE CONGO

> '*Tshombe is a turncoat, a traitor to the interests of the Congolese people. If one compares Tshombe with his counterpart in the revolution in our own country he is a Petlyura. Mr Hammarskjöld, on behalf of the United Nations, is backing in the Congo Colonel Mobutu, who is acting against the Congolese Government. But Mobutu is a highwayman. If we search for an analogy in our own country, it is something like a Wrangel, Kolchak, or similar flotsam of history which our people chucked out.*'
>
> NIKITA KHRUSCHEV, 27 September 1960

As usually happens in African controversies, the West found itself divided over the Congo. But this time the rift was small, with Belgium the odd man out, relying only on France's sympathetic support; this did not amount to much – except that it gave France's enemies in Africa fresh ammunition. Portugal hardly counted.

THE ROLE OF THE WEST

France's role in the UN was largely confined to abstaining from any proposition touching the Congo. When the UN closed down Leopoldville Radio, Kasavubu was allowed to use Radio Congo in Brazzaville. Ghana has officially accused France of going behind the back of the UN on the grounds that Radio Brazzaville is, by treaty, still controlled by the French. But this accusation is based on a misunderstanding explained in a footnote on the previous page.

The Western approach, as could be expected, showed the same unwillingness to be too hard on one of its allies as it shows to France over Algeria, and, sometimes, towards South Africa over South West Africa. But, understandable as it is that allies should not wish to wound each other on issues that temporarily divide them, the West should not be surprised if its actions in the non-committed world are viewed with some suspicion so long as its internal dilemmas remain unreconciled.

France, Belgium, and Portugal aside, the rest of the West were broadly united; their agreement was expressed through general support for the line taken by the Afro-Asian group. The explanation of this remarkable line-up is that, for once, Western interests happened to coincide with those of the non-committed nations. Both groups wish to keep the cold war out of the Congo, though not necessarily for the same reasons. It was inevitable that this community of interest should have looked like 'ganging up' against the Soviet *bloc*, which found itself isolated in the Security Council, with the Western nations (Belgium and France excepted) supporting the resolutions put forward by the Afro-Asians.

Although the Western *bloc* showed a notable softness towards the Belgians, they did not equivocate on the main issues in the Congo. While they did what they could to dissuade the Afro-Asians from presenting too sharply-worded resolutions to the Security Council, they also used their influence on the Belgians to dissuade them from pursuing some of their more extreme policies. For example, the Western nations firmly refused to play Belgium's game when she sought recognition for Katanga's independent status; only France equivocated. They succeeded in persuading Belgium herself not to grant such recognition to Katanga. Even when Belgium threatened to withdraw from NATO, the West stood firm.

There is no other recent example when the West played so passive a role in international affairs as it did in the Congo. It was not that the Western States had no interests. Politically, Portugal and the Central African Federation (hence, by implication, Britain) might easily have found themselves in an awkward position, had events turned out differently. Economically, Britain and the United States shared large interests with the Belgians.

The classic analysis of imperialism would lead one to conclude that the 'colonialists' would have banded together to safeguard their interests. The Soviet *bloc* operated on this theory; but their theoretical approach led them into serious difficulties because it failed to recognize the new relationships that have been developing between the former colonial powers and the newly-independent states as a result of decolonization.

The Belgians imperilled their future economic relations with the Congo, but there was no such threat to the other Western Powers. Indeed some of them, notably the United States, stood to gain considerably from the Congo's independence. Patrice Lumumba, when he was Prime Minister, negotiated an agreement for the joint development of the Congo's resources by the Congo Government and the Congo International Management Corporation, headed by the American financier, L. Edgar Detwiler, who was supported by important Wall Street interests, and who claimed also to have the support of the State Department. This £700-million deal was held up only because Lumumba's Cabinet refused to approve the contract signed by their Prime Minister. Right up to the time he was deposed, Lumumba continued to urge this deal on his Cabinet. Powerful American financial circles, therefore, had every reason to desire a strengthening of Lumumba's position, and the restoration of his Government's authority over Katanga.

Not all financial interests in America or Britain were equally content however. Those who had close Belgian ties were alarmed at the prospect of their losses if the Belgians should finally lose all influence in the Congo; they were also afraid that new financiers, like Detwiler, would be involved in 'take-over' bids with the Congo Government. But although several powerful financial interests, especially American, colluded with the Belgians, they were unable to influence American and Western policies, which never once came into conflict with the policies of the non-committed nations.

The British attitude to the policy followed by the majority of the African States was summed up by Mr Sandys, the Minister for Commonwealth Relations, in September: 'The world owes President Nkrumah a considerable debt for the statesmanlike way he has approached the crisis in the Congo.'

BELGIUM'S ROLE

If the Congo became a happy hunting-ground for the Soviet *bloc*, at least for a time, the responsibility is Belgium's. Her attempts to recover from her mistakes led to a succession of crises which produced chaos and finally opened the way for the increasingly isolated and frustrated Congo Prime Minister to turn to the Russians. In this way, the Belgians, who had the most to fear from Russian influence in the Congo, contributed most to its growth.

Belgium's role in the Congo, after the UN decision to intervene, greatly harmed her true interests, and those of her allies. It is possible to make excuses for her decision to commit her troops in the first place; but the subsequent behaviour of the Belgians is less easy to excuse. They misled Hammarskjöld into believing that all their troops had been withdrawn from Katanga, when, in fact, they knew this was not so. Hammarskjöld critiiczed them severely for their deception. Not only did they staff Tshombe's Government, but they allowed 'volunteers' from the Belgian Army to stiffen his army, thus maintaining the reality of the Belgian presence in the Congo. When they were finally compelled to withdraw from their bases in Katanga (having unsuccessfully tried to argue that these were not covered by the Security Council resolution), they transferred large quantities of arms and supplies to the Katanga Army. This was done at a time when the UN was insisting that no military supplies should be sent directly to the Central Government.

The Belgians deliberately built up Katanga's military strength. The extent of Belgian aid, disclosed by authoritative sources to Eric Kennedy of the London *Daily Mail** showed that, between 11 July (the day on which Tshombe set up his state) and 8 September, more than 100 tons of arms and ammunition were flown from Brussels to Katanga, including mortars, sub-machine guns, and FN-38 automatic rifles. (This was in addition to the supplies transferred from their Congo bases.) Twenty-five Belgian Air Force planes were repainted with Katanga's colours. Eighty-nine Belgian officers and NCOs, serving with the Force Publique, were seconded to Tshombe's Army, in addition to 326 Belgian NCOs and technicians who are serving as 'volunteers'. At the beginning of September a further seventy Belgian officers, NCOs, and members of the *gendarmerie* were despatched from Brussels. The UN finally put an end to these reinforcements by closing Elizabethville airport on 8 September.

The Belgian-officered force of Katanga volunteers came into

* *Daily Mail*, 9 September 1960.

armed conflict with UN troops in the third week of September when they set out to capture Luluabourg, the capital of Kasai. General Indarjit Rikhye, the Indian military adviser to Hammarskjöld, reported severe casualties before the invaders were persuaded to withdraw. He disclosed that they were supplied by jet helicopters and planes from Katanga; the troops were armed with modern weapons. Belgian policy in the Congo therefore continues to represent a threat to the country's integrity.

Criticism of Belgian policy is not confined to outside critics; at home the Government has been hard pressed by influential Belgians. The nature and tone of these criticisms are shown by the speech of M. Victor Larock, deputy, former Foreign Minister, and member of the Belgian Socialist Party Executive, when he moved a motion of no confidence in the Government.*

It is largely the fault of the Belgian Government that Belgium is held in discredit by virtually the whole of the world. . . . The prestige of Belgium in the world has fallen – it could not be lower. . . . The Congo was lost to Belgium not on 30 June, but in the succeeding period, when Belgians had become undesirables in the Congo and Belgium suspect in the United Nations. At the time of the first resolution of the Security Council the Government had two choices – unreserved compliance with the resolution, or following the 'ultras' whose only concern is their investments and who look only to the force of arms to save them. The Government tried to combine the two attitudes. It gave an affirmative reply to the UN, but it failed to repudiate the policy of force, trying to satisfy the champions of force, by devious interpretations of texts, ambiguous statements, and unjustified delays. From the onset of the mutinies the Government shilly-shallied and committed unpardonable blunders.

M. Larock added:

The 'ultras' had one obsession – to save their financial stake in the country. We Socialists are not indifferent to the fact that the greater part of the Congo is not viable without Katanga, nor to the fact that the Mining Combine contributes three milliards of francs annually to the Belgian Exchequer. What revolts Socialists is the hypocrisy of concealing – with humanitarian, civic, or moral pretexts – interests which are not named, but which all Belgium and all the world can point a finger to. . . . The big idea of the 'ultras' was to reform the

* Belgian Chamber of Deputies, 17 August 1960.

Congo, beginning with the Katanga, but first to provoke its break-up.
... The Government should have acted firmly. ... To encourage
secession and then, as a result, to favour a split-up of the Congo was
no way to save what could and should have been saved in Katanga, in
the interests of the Belgians and the Congolese alike. Once it had been
reconstituted, the Congo would have become the prey of foreign capital-
ism, looking for the best titbits. ... The lack of loyalty to the UN has
done harm to our cause. I accuse the Government of having acted in
such a way as to make it appear that Belgium was indifferent to her duty
to the UN, and was much too grief-stricken by its financial losses. ...
Nobody knows where the Congo is heading. If it is to anarchy and
disintegration, the policy of the Government will have contributed ...
the responsibility for the present disaster lies at the feet of the present
Government. Never has our country been so isolated under the burden
of the mistakes committed in her name.

SOVIET INTERVENTION

The Congo gave the Soviet *bloc* their first real taste of African
politics. They made just about every mistake in the book, and
when they were finally forced out, their emissaries were happy to
leave; personal accounts of their experiences were bitter. One
prominent Polish emissary said: 'We might as well have been
Belgians.'

The Soviet *bloc* found itself at an initial disadvantage, with few
friends or allies through whom to work. At the UN they were
faced with a solid *bloc* of African and Asian States unwilling to
yield to either of the power *blocs*. In the Congo they found two
Ministers, Anicet Kashamuru, the Minister of Information, and
Antoine Gizenga, the vice-Premier, willing to offer them an outlet
for some of their propaganda; but though both are described as
Marxists, neither is a Muscovite. At first Lumumba was coldly
hostile to them. It should be recalled that his first appeal for aid
went to Washington; his second to the UN; his third to the Bandung Powers; his fourth to the African States. It was only in a
final state of despair that he decided to use Russian aid.

Lumumba's decision to ask for Russian aid, and Russia's
decision to supply it, cannot be questioned on legal grounds;
their rights are clearly established. The only point at issue is
whether Russian actions conflicted with the Security Council's

decisions. In a Note on 5 September, Hammarskjöld alleged they did. The Russians rejected this charge on the grounds that the first resolution of 14 July did not restrict, and could not restrict, the right of the government of a sovereign state to request assistance from the governments of other countries; nor did it give UN officials the right to control any assistance given. The Russians' position on this point is unquestionably right. But the Security Council's second decision urged all states to refrain from actions which might hamper the restoration of law and order, and the exercise of its authority by the Congo government; and also to refrain from action that might undermine the Republic's territorial integrity and political independence. The Russians claimed they were assisting the Congo government to fulfil these purposes. The supply of civil aircraft and motor vehicles 'far from running counter to the resolutions of the Security Council, is completely in accordance with them'.

The Russian claim that their aid assisted the Central Government to carry out its policies is, of course, true. Their aid was used to put down the revolt of the 'Diamond State'. Without the help of Russian transport, Lumumba could not have undertaken that mission, since all planes and other suitable transport in the country were in the hands of the UN, whose Command would not allow them to be used against the rebel government. Whether UN policy was right on this question will be considered separately. What is relevant here is to recognize that the Russians chose to operate outside the framework of the UN, thereby diminishing its authority and control. The Russians did not seek the approval of the African States for their action. On the contrary, when the matter came before the Security Council the African group insisted that all aid to the Congo should be channelled through the UN.

Although the Russians can fairly claim to have acted in response to a legal government, which had the right to summon its aid, their action was clearly intended to flout the UN authority; this was consistent with their view that UN policy in the Congo was insupportable. They were critical of the UN Command, and thought its policies served the 'colonialists', while discriminating against the Russians. They relied on one element to justify their allegations of bias. The UN had relied mainly on British and

American planes, with civilian crews, to fly troops to the Congo. The Russians were not asked to make their planes available. When they did use them to fly Ghana troops to the Congo, Hammarskjöld protested on the grounds that all troop-carrying had to be routed through UN controls. This principle is obviously of vital importance. But would the UN position not have been less assailable had he also invited the Russians to supply planes with civilian crews?

Russia's long, losing battles in the Security Council have already been described. The basis of her policy, and her criticisms of UN policy, still need to be considered. The Soviet case rested on the premise that UN intervention amounted to 'a coalition of colonialists which aims to suppress the young African state by the hands of African soldiers from Tunisia, Morocco, Ethiopia, and Ghana'.* The Russian attempt to isolate these four is the closest they came to suggesting the African States were the stooges of the colonialists. The detailed charges pressed against the UN by the Russians are contained in the following summary of a speech delivered by Valerian Zorin to the emergency session of the UN General Assembly on 17 September.

Having put itself at the head of a conspiracy against the young African State, the United States had waited for its subversive activities to bring down a government for which it felt a fierce hatred, as did the other colonial powers. That hatred arose from the fact that the Lumumba Government had been so bold as to adopt a policy of consolidating its country's independence and of getting rid, not only of the Belgian colonialists, but also of all other colonialists. The Lumumba Government's patriotic policy endangered the position of the colonialist powers in the Congo, including those of the United States – powers which are vitally interested in retaining control over the extremely rich resources of the Congo. The tragic developments were a direct outgrowth of the criminal activities of a coalition led by the United States. That coalition had succeeded in using the United Nations Command and Secretary-General Hammarskjöld in person for its own ends. The sad upshot of the operations of the UN Command and the Secretary-General is that the territorial integrity of the Republic of the Congo, far from being restored, is being exposed to an

* Statement by the Soviet Government, 9 September 1960.

even greater threat today than it was two months ago. .... The final effect of their action in the Congo – action which should have been aimed at providing assistance to the legal government of that country – was the removal of that government, and what looks like the physical extermination of its leaders. The Secretary-General became a party to a farce which took the form of an open crime. For the rest, the charge seeks to establish a direct link between Belgium and its NATO allies in Katanga and in the rest of the country.

Leaving aside the overtones of cold war politics, what truth is there in the Soviet allegations? Was the United States the prime mover in the 'coalition of colonialists' against whom Lumumba sought to act? Lumumba never criticized American policy in the Congo, either directly or indirectly. Far from showing any desire to remove the control of Congo resources from the U.S., Lumumba's 'patriotic policy' was to try to force through his deal with the American financier Detwiler against the overwhelming opposition from his Cabinet.

Was Hammarskjöld the agent of the 'colonialist coalition'? Some of his mistakes have already been mentioned; others will be considered in the final chapter. Hammarskjöld's policies were considered by the Security Council on four separate occasions; each time they upheld him. Only once did the Russians seek to oppose a Security Council decision. This led to a direct appeal to the UN General Assembly. His policies were endorsed by seventy votes to nil.

What logical deductions can be made from these decisions? All the resolutions passed by both the Assembly and the Council were formulated by the African group and endorsed by the Asian group. Are they therefore the agents of the colonialists? Although the Soviet *bloc* has never said as much (except for the incautious reference to Ghana, Tunisia, Morocco, and Ethiopia referred to earlier), this really is their view of the governments of the present African and Asian states (excluding possibly only Guinea and the U.A.R.). Their difficulty is that it is politically inconvenient for them to say so too openly, especially when the Africans act in unison.

Is the Security Council the agent of the colonialists? The Council's decision, challenged by the Russians, was upheld by the whole of the UN Assembly, with the Soviet *bloc* dissenting. Neither the U.A.R. nor Guinea; neither Yugoslavia nor Indonesia; neither India nor Iraq, upheld the Russian objections. The only logical conclusion, therefore, is that the entire UN (barring only the Soviet *bloc*) is in the camp of the colonialists.

We are left with one final allegation: that the UN was responsible for overthrowing the Lumumba Government. The evidence for this has already been discussed in the last chapter. The African States believe that mistakes were made by the UN, but they have never suggested that the UN had sought to overthrow the Lumumba Government. Dr Nkrumah's* summing up was 'that it would be entirely wrong to blame either the Security Council or any senior officials of the UN for what had taken place . . . these difficulties are in essence the growing pains of the UN.' Presented with a choice of verdicts on this question – that of the Soviet *bloc*, and that of the African group – it is not difficult to come to a decision. However, it is one thing to say that the UN did not deliberately seek to overthrow the Lumumba Government, and quite another to suggest that the combination of its policies and its mistakes did not help to produce this result.

* Address to the UN General Assembly, 23 September 1960.

Chapter 16

SUMMING-UP

'The UN Force in the Congo is the most advanced and the most sophisticated experiment in international cooperation ever attempted . . . among all that is so sad and so mean and so sour in world politics it is heartening to think that something so good and so pure in its purpose is possible.'

WALTER LIPPMANN

THE fortunes of the UN in the Congo depended on several factors. The most important was the internal political struggle. The most helpful was the role of the African States. The least helpful were Belgian and Soviet policies. The balancing factor was the character and capacity of the UN Secretary-General, Dag Hammarskjöld, and the quality of his staff. None of these factors operated individually; yet each, except for the Soviet factor, was capable of destroying the international effort. Bearing these in mind, two conditions were necessary for success – to secure and maintain UN agreement; and to mobilize an international army and administration capable of running the country in harmony with the wishes of its political leaders. At the time of writing, the UN intervention in the Congo is still in the balance; all that can be done here is to examine the success and the failure of its role up to the end of October 1960.

UN BALANCE SHEET

UN intervention in the Congo was intended to achieve five aims. The first was to expel the Belgian troops. This aim was achieved; but it stopped short of expelling Belgians seconded to the Katanga Army. This failure left open a backdoor through which hundreds of Belgian reinforcements returned as 'volunteers' before the UN finally shut down Katanga's airports.

The second aim was to provide the Central Government with

military assistance until their own national security forces could fully meet their tasks. Such assistance was provided. More than 19,000 troops from fourteen countries (ten of them African) were brought in. They dealt with civil disturbances, maintenance of essential services, protection of refugees and minorities; they used their good offices in situations ranging from tribal war to arbitrary arrest of individuals; they maintained a pacification line between Katanga and the rest of the Congo; and they made a start with forming and training a national army. But from the first there was no agreement between the UN Command and the army commanders on the role of the troops in relation to the Force Publique. General Alexander, acting under the authority of the Ghana Government, wanted to disarm the entire Force temporarily as a prelude to establishing discipline and reforming it into a national army. This was not the view of the UN Command. It saw its task as a 'peace force' which should not even temporarily replace the Force Publique. Its role was to separate contesting foes. The theory is that 'keeping the peace' creates the chance of peaceful negotiations. Few will quarrel with this theory. But if the UN Force was to be restricted to a purely 'non-intervention' role, how was the UN's third aim – restoring the unity of the Congo – to be met? The weakness of UN policy was not that it ruled out a forcible solution but that in a situation that demanded a settlement it provided no alternatives.

The fourth aim was to provide technical assistance to enable the Government to function. It made gigantic efforts to meet this obligation. Had it not been for the collapse of all effective authority, which largely confined the UN to providing emergency services, its contribution in this field might have been – perhaps it might still become – its greatest achievement.

The fifth aim – to keep the cold war out of Africa – was also not achieved. The Russians were used by Lumumba; and the Soviet *bloc* turned the Congo into a major cold war incident by indicting the Secretary-General for his 'lack of impartiality'. This became the Russian pretext for demanding the reorganization of the UN Secretariat to reflect the division of the world into three *blocs*: Western, communist, and non-committed.

CRUCIAL ERRORS

The analysis thus far leaves out of account the 'hot blood' of Congolese realities. To cast all the blame for what went wrong on the UN is demonstrably false; equally, to ignore its mistakes is to falsify the facts.

In retrospect it is much easier to see where the UN went wrong. It made three crucial errors all of which stem from the doctrine of 'non-intervention'. It made no effort to restore the unity of the Congo. It acted with equal impartiality towards the legal and the rebel governments. And it failed to deal effectively with the Force Publique.

The Central Government originally sought UN intervention on specific issues affecting its internal affairs: to train a national army; to set up a civil service; to maintain security; to uphold the country's integrity. The UN accepted all these obligations; nevertheless it insisted on being guided by its own policies as to how they should be fulfilled. This was both natural and proper. But in fulfilling these obligations it sometimes allowed itself to intervene in matters of clearly domestic concern – for example its decision to close down the Leopoldville radio station and to keep control over the airports at all times – while at other times it took refuge behind 'non-intervention'.

The guiding principle of 'non-intervention' established by the Charter of the UN, was re-affirmed by the Security Council in its resolution of 9 August 1960, which specified that the UN Force in the Congo 'would not be a party to, or in any way intervene in, or be used to influence the outcome of, any internal conflict, constitutional or otherwise'. This was also the view of the African States.

That 'non-intervention' was never possible is admitted even by the UN Organization for the Congo*: 'It is manifest that the decision of the Security Council, in acceding to a governmental request for military assistance to the national security forces in the restoration of law and order, has itself automatically juxtaposed the international and domestic spheres of action.' The Organization also admits that 'it was already a difficult and

---

* Progress Report, 20 September 1960.

delicate task ... in the period from the date of its first entry up to the end of August 1960, to exercise its responsibility for maintaining peace and security without impinging an any internal function of government. By mid-September, however, the constitutional crises had resulted in the breakdown of the formal structure of government into partially overlapping but largely competitive power groups. ... In such circumstances actions undertaken by the UN tended to become a bone of contention with one internal group or another.'

The fallacy of the doctrine of 'non-intervention' in the Congo derives from the mistaken concept that the situation was analogous to previous interventions by the UN Force where, as a peace force, it could stop two antagonists getting at each other's throats. But this was not possible in the Congo, where the situation demanded active intervention on the side of the Government.

THE FIRST MISTAKE

UN policy on Katanga* rested on two principles. The first was that the UN Force could not be used to subdue Tshombe's Government by force. The other was that the UN had no right to refuse the Central Government to intervene in Katanga.

This policy left the initiative for restoring the country's integrity entirely to Lumumba. In the circumstances he could deal with this situation in one of two ways: either to appeal for help outside the UN, or to negotiate a settlement with Tshombe (and later with Kalonji in the 'Diamond State') on the only basis they were willing to consider – the concession of a federal solution. The Government refused to negotiate on these terms. Criticisms of its actions must be political judgements, not legal verdicts.

The African States did their best to persuade Lumumba to act differently, but the Prime Minister chose to ignore negotiations, to use Russian aid, and to attack the 'Diamond State' as the first step towards re-establishing the Congo's integrity. The consequences of this action were disastrous for him. It destroyed national unity, and it wrecked his Government. The result was that the Government which the UN had agreed to support disintegrated, with appalling repercussions. It is ridiculous to blame

* See page 136.

the UN for Lumumba's mistakes. But his mistakes came from his attempt to restore the integrity of the Congo. It was the wrong way, but he was within his rights to act as he did.

There were only two ways of preventing his actions: either the UN could taken the initiative in restoring the Congo's unity or it could have insisted on peaceful negotiation. The first alternative was ruled out by its own policies. To have insisted on the second would have been gross interference in an internal question, since the issue of federalism or unitarianism was the nub of Congo political divisions.

The total effect of UN policy in Katanga was to freeze the position in Tshombe's favour. It failed to take sufficiently into account the dangers the Katanga threat held for the rest of the Congo. Katanga's continued existence as an independent state, resting on Belgian arms and support, was as lively a threat to the integrity and security of the rest of the Congo as if it had been, in fact, engaged in open hostilities with the Central Government. Here was a colonial base in which the Belgians were openly working for the dismemberment of the Congo, and for the downfall of the Lumumba Government.

The longer Katanga survived as an independent state, the stronger its encouragement to others to follow its example. The 'Diamond State' of Kasai tried to follow its example. It received active support from Katanga when it proclaimed its independence. When this happened there were signs that other regions might follow the examples of Katanga and the 'Diamond State'. What was the Central Government to do when the rot began to spread from the Belgian-supported Katanga to the rest of the country? Its ability to assert its weak authority was even further weakened; confidence was sapped; and the political leaders were prevented from concentrating their efforts on governing the country. The divisions inside the coalition widened, with the federalists encouraged to press their demands against the unitarians. Simply to ignore these problems and to pretend that Lumumba was just an irresponsible madman hardly squares with the facts as they must have appeared to him.

The case for not acting against Katanga should also be considered. In the early stages of the crisis Katanga was the only oasis of relative tranquillity in a sea of chaos. It would have been no easy task to persuade the UN to extend the area of conflict. But any realistic assessment of the situation in Katanga would have shown that its tranquillity was illusory; it could not possibly survive for long. Sooner or later, unless there was a peaceful solution, which became increasingly remote, it would have been overwhelmed by the Congo's legal Government. Meanwhile, it was contributing actively towards creating instability in the Congo. The Belgian presence strengthened the rebel Government, and induced rebellion against Lumumba's. For example, it was Belgian 'volunteers', arms, and supplies which made possible the Baluba march on Luluabourg, the capital of Kasai.*

While forcibly putting the position of the Congolese, it must be remembered that the UN has its own difficulties. It is not free to act as it wishes. It is circumscribed by its own conventions and conditioned by the nature of its membership. This much is conceded; but only to emphasize the need for a revision of UN concepts. In the Congo, the Secretary-General could have avoided many of his personal difficulties if, from the beginning, he had established a Regional Advisory Council of African States to work with the UN Organization. His later attempt to set up an Advisory Council shows that he had recognized the value of this concept. But his action suffered from two defects. It came too late, and it included two European States, on the grounds that they were contributing to the UN Force; this weakened its value as an impartial sanctioning authority.

THE SECOND MISTAKE

UN policy suffered from one other, almost fatal defect. It made no apparent distinction between legality and illegality in the Congo. Dr Nkrumah's analysis† of where the UN went wrong deserves attention. 'Certain propositions seem to me to be self-evident,' he said. 'The first of these is that the UN need not to go to the assistance of any country which invites its intervention. But once it has done so, it owes an obligation to the Government and people of that country not to interfere in such a way as to prevent the legitimate Government which invited it to enter the country

* See page 160.
† Address to the UN General Assembly, 23 September.

from fulfilling its mandate. In other words, it is impossible for the UN at one and the same time to preserve law and order and to be neutral between the legal authorities and the law-breakers. It is, unfortunately, exactly this which the UN has attempted to do in the case of the Congo, and which is the cause of all the present difficulties and disagreements. My second proposition is that in any sovereign state there can only be one national army. If a soldier disobeys his superior officer and uses his arms to murder and loot, he is a mutineer. There is, however, no difference between his position and that of a colonel who disregards the authority which appointed him and uses the troops under his own command for his own purposes. The UN, in enforcing law and order, must deal equally sternly with either of these two types of mutineer. This failure by the UN to distinguish between legal and illegal authorities led to the most ludicrous results. . . .'

THE THIRD MISTAKE

The failure to discipline and reorganize the Force Publique, and to bring the new army under the temporary supervision of the UN Command, was crucial. The Security Council resolution called for the creation of a national army. Such an army could only have been created if the Katanga Army had been brought under the control of the UN and peacefully integrated into the new force. The UN made not the slightest effort to give effect to this part of its resolution; the result was that Tshombe's army remained intact and could be strengthened almost at will by the Belgians, until the UN finally closed the airports.

Had the Force Publique been temporarily disarmed and then reorganized, it would not have been possible for Lumumba to have launched his campaign on the 'Diamond State' of Kasai. Nor would it have been possible, later, for Colonel Mobutu to have overthrown all forms of parliamentary government. To have escaped only these last two developments would have added considerably to the security and stability of the Congo.

Although there was a time – after Lumumba mistakenly thought he had gained control over the Force Publique – when it would have been difficult to have acted along these lines, two opportunities were missed. The first was when the Ghana troops,

under General Alexander, began to operate along this policy and
were opposed by the UN Commander. The second opportunity
came after the collapse of the Central Government when the
Force was used against parliament. But the UN doctrine of 'the
peace force' ruled out any policy of this kind. The question that
must be considered in case of future 'Congos' is whether this
approach is compatible with the UN's undertaking obligations
such as it did in the Congo.

OTHER WEAKNESSES

The UN was obviously unprepared to deal with the swift and
gathering responsibilities thrust on it by the Congo. In its rush to
develop a scratch administration it failed to field a balanced team
of experts representing all the major elements in its membership.
This failure, however understandable, must cause misunderstanding, especially when two-thirds of the staff recruited for the
Congo administration, was drawn from Western countries. In
assessing what weight to give to the Russian's criticisms on this
point it is necessary to remember their refusal to contribute to
the UN technical personnel; a policy they have deliberately fostered.
Soviet bloc countries asked by Hammarskjöld to provide technical personnel for the Congo refused his requests.

The UN Organization in the Congo was also sadly lacking in
experts with experience in African politics; there is a world of
difference between an African expert and an expert in problems
of African Government. The result was that the Organization
misjudged the political forces in the country and, at times, appears
to have been guided by wishful thinking rather than by accurate
diagnosis. It was always possible for Hammarskjöld to have
asked for a dozen senior African civil servants to be seconded to
his staff. As far as I know he had only two such persons in senior
posts.

CONCLUSION

At the time of writing, the UN has failed to maintain the two
conditions established earlier for the success of its operation. It
failed to maintain agreement within the UN, and it failed to

establish administrative and armed forces capable of working in harmony with the wishes of the political leaders. These failures do not stem only from the mistakes of the UN. Cold war politicians could always find a way round the most impartial of policies; but their tactics in the Congo thrived on the UN's mistakes and difficulties. Nor is it possible to establish harmony with political leaders unless they are broadly united in their wishes. This condition existed at the beginning at the UN operation, but it was unfortunately lost later.

To criticize the UN is an act of faith. Unless disaster follows disaster in the ill-starred Congo, there is still reason to believe that, before the last chapter is written in the Congo story, the UN will have overcome its initial difficulties; the Belgians will have come to understand how short-sightedly they have behaved; and the Congolese will have found their true destiny in Africa, endowed as they are with a rich cultural heritage and with great potential wealth.